Amending a Commercial Lease

Third Edition

For Sam, Tom and Jack.
Live your life Boys.

Amending a Commercial Lease

Third Edition

Karl Bamford

LLB (Hons), Partner at Knight & Sons,
Newcastle-under-Lyme, Staffordshire
www.knightandsons.co.uk

The images on the front cover of this book show Knight & Sons offices at The Brampton, Newcastle-under-Lyme, Staffs; www.knightandsons.co.uk

Tottel
publishing

TOTTEL PUBLISHING LTD, MAXWELTON HOUSE, 41–43 BOLTRO ROAD, HAYWARDS HEATH, WEST SUSSEX, RH16 1BJ

© Tottel Publishing Ltd 2007

A CIP Catalogue record for this book is available from the British Library.

ISBN 13 978 1 84592 235 1

ISBN 10 1 84592 235 2

Typeset by Phoenix Photosetting, Chatham, Kent

Printed and bound in Great Britain by M & A Thomson Litho, East Kilbride, Glasgow

Preface

Time marches on. Someone once said it waits for no one; in particular certainly not for busy property lawyers who now operate in a fast, dynamic and quickly changing marketplace. There have been many changes to legislation and practice since the last Edition in January 2003 – I can scarcely believe it is over three years since the Second Edition was published. These three years have probably seen more changes in practice and procedures than all my previous years in practice.

The marketplace initiated the changes and was the catalyst. Oversupply of property and falling rents led landlords to review their operating practices; punitive concepts (privity of contract etc.) leading to financial hardship for many tenants and suddenly politicians and legislators were interested in the property world. No doubt motivated by heavy constituency postbags full of letters from disgruntled tenants, they decided to have their say.

The politicians responded with the Code of Practice (set out later in the text) and the balance of power between landlords and tenants slowly began to shift. Gently at first, but the trickle soon became a stream and that stream (whilst not yet a fully fledged river) certainly has a momentum which a few years ago was inconceivable.

Suddenly the tenant has power. Power in the marketplace; landlords who had previously proved totally intransigent were having to consider flexibility on lease terms. Suddenly everything is up for negotiation. Legal practice and procedure can at times be clumsy and slothful in reflecting such changes and advisors must be mindful of this and nimble with pen or keyboard! Negotiating a commercial lease has never been more challenging or, indeed, more fun (if you want to view it like that!). It is up to tenants' advisers to make as much use of this current climate as they possibly can. Do not be timid. Start as you mean to go on and set out the rules of negotiation as early as you can. Explain in detail the consequences to your clients of agreeing to certain standard provisions in Heads of Terms (full repairing, upward only rent reviews etc) and take these challenges head on. Even better, if possible, try and educate clients to involve you in the Heads of Terms process; it will save time and later irritation.

New legislation continues to be introduced which affects the negotiation of commercial leases. Landlords and tenants need to be aware of their obligations under the Disability Discrimination Act of 1995 as amended by the Disability Discrimination Act 2005 which comes into force on 4 December 2006 and imposes obligations on landlords and managers of leased premises. The impact of the Landlord and Tenant (Covenants) Act 1995 is now well established. There is now case law guidance on the interpretations of the provisions of this particular piece of legislation of which practitioners need to be aware when finalising leases. In consequence of the introduction of stamp duty land tax by the Finance Act 2003 (with effect from 1 December 2004) the tenant needs to be advised of his liability in this respect. Is a proposed longer lease with a tenant's break option better restructured as a shorter-term lease coupled with a tenant's option to renew to make it more tax efficient? Involve accountants and surveyors in the process.

Tenants should be made aware of the fact that by virtue of the Land Registration Act 2002 a lease will require registration at the HM Land Registry if the term of the lease is more than seven years, or is granted more than three months before it is to take effect, however short the term may be, or is a lease under which the right to possession is discontinuous (for example a timeshare lease) under the Landlord & Tenant Act 1954 by virtue of the Regulatory Reform (Business Tenancies) (England & Wales) Order 2003, advisers need to be conscious of the changes to the procedures for contracting out, lease termination and lease renewals.

It may be important for the parties to consider whether the lease should be designated as an exempt information document (see the commentary on clause 3.9.4 in the lease).

A lot of people have worked hard to help in the production of this new Edition. Firstly, to my friend (and Consultant at Knight & Sons) Tony Bell whose thirst for knowledge in the world of property law shows no signs of abating. He is such a wonderful source of energy, enthusiasm and drive; he puts many of us to shame. He leads with a guiding hand that, quite frankly, I am not sure I would know what to do without! He is a true inspiration in so many ways. But mostly he is just a great man. Cheers Boss!

Once again, a huge debt of gratitude to my secretary, Michelle Elphinstone-Walker for her selfless devotion of time in helping prepare the manuscripts and all her general duties. She has suffered me now for over ten years and I hope many more. She has had a difficult year but has borne it with courage and her usual selflessness. She is a wonderful friend.

To all my friends and colleagues at Knight & Sons which continues to flourish both as a wonderful, progressive, dynamic and challenging legal firm and as an environment within which people are allowed to flourish free of worry and the dreadful pressures many who work in the law suffer. The partners deserve a great deal of credit for this. In particular, our senior partner, Derek Miller. A more caring and compassionate man you will not find, a true friend in every sense.

To my editor, Andy Hill, for his compassionate understanding of my failure to meet deadlines and his patient forbearance as days became weeks and weeks become months! It's been a difficult year, so thanks Andy, I hope you think it was worth the wait.

Finally, to Sam, Tom and Jack, the reason I do most things these days. Three fine young men of whom I am so proud. I love you boys.

Karl Bamford
Alsager
Stoke-on-Trent
August 2006

Contents

Table of statutes

Table of statutory instruments

Table of cases

Note on the Code of Practice for Commercial Leases

In the author's view, the most radical changes to the structure of commercial leases has been brought about in consequence of the second edition of the Code of Practice for Commercial Leases in England and Wales, which is set out in its entirety at page xvii. This second edition of the Code was published in April 2002, and was greeted with considerably more attention than the first. Both the landlord and tenant should have regard to the recommendations contained in the Code. At the launch of the Code in April 2002, the government did state that, if there was no evidence at the end of a period of two years that the recommendations in the Code were being adopted, legislation would follow. From a landlord's point of view a lease which does not comply with the Code may result in a lower rent on the grant of the lease, on rent review and also on lease renewal and, it is suggested, therefore that a landlord's solicitor should make his client aware of the provisions of the Code and the possible effect of non-compliance with this. From the tenant's point of view the Code should give his surveyor and/or solicitor leverage in seeking amendments to a draft lease which contains provisions which are contrary to the recommendations of the Code. It will also be relevant for the provisions of the Code to be considered and taken into account by the tenant's advisers on rent review and lease renewal, in seeking to negotiate a lower rent to reflect any onerous or restrictive provisions in the lease that are contrary to the recommendations in the Code.

The author knows for a fact that the Prudential took on board the Code's recommendations lock, stock and barrel in relation to its commercial lettings and, as will be seen from the recommendations, some of these are quite radical and mark quite a departure from what is considered to be the current commercial norm in lease negotiations and lease structures.

Broadly speaking, the recommendations break down into three types:

1.   The first type relates to the negotiating process for commercial leases. Many of the recommendations are simply good business practice, which many investors already follow, but there are others which, perhaps, are not likely to prove to be as palatable to landlords, as they involve giving tenants a choice as to the length of term including break clauses where appropriate, and if alternative lease terms can be offered, differential rents. Commercial reality, the author believes, means that it is always going to be difficult to price an alternative set of terms.

2.   The second type of recommendations put forward by the Code relates
        to the behaviour of the parties during the lifetime of the lease. An exam-
        ple of this is a guarantor who will now be expected to agree (or not, as
        the case may be!) to any material changes to the terms of the lease.

3.   The third and final type of recommendations puts forward specific
        changes to investor leases, and areas dealt with are as follows:

● Insurance

● Alienation – Assignment

● Alterations

Whilst I will attempt in this work to highlight those areas of the lease which
will be affected by the Code's recommendations by referring to the relevant
recommendations in the Commentary, I would strongly urge practitioners to
familiarise themselves with the Code's recommendations, because it is the
author's view that these proposals will see a radical shift in how leases are
negotiated, and ignorance of or indifference towards these recommendations
may well cause difficulties for, and indeed bad advice being given by, those
attempting to settle any future commercial leases.

In the light of the interim report of Reading University published in April
2004, which reported that the Code was having little effect on leasing practices, the government immediately launched an early consultation exercise
focusing on whether upwards only rent reviews should be abolished with six
possible options being set out in the consultation document. The government
stated that they would decide whether to legislate after consideration of both
the outcome of the consultation process and also the final report of Reading
University, which was published on 24 February 2005. This report – and this
will come as no surprise – found that, where a lease contains a rent review
clause, the rent review is almost always upwards. They also found that tenants' awareness of the Code is relatively low and that the Code is having little
effect on individual lease negotiations.

The Office of the Deputy Prime Minister issued a written ministerial statement on 15 March 2005, following consideration of the final report of
Reading University and their own consultation exercise on upward only rent
review clauses. As regards upwards only rent review clauses they stated that
they did not propose at present to legislate against such clauses, but that they
would continue to monitor the situation and retain the option to legislate in
the future if necessary. The period of the further monitoring exercise is three
years. However, the ministerial statement picked up on the fact that 'major
problems are inflexible assignment and subletting provisions', and their intention therefore is 'to undertake a review of the law of assignment and subletting with the aim of easing the position for tenants while not jeopardising
property investment, including looking at legislative options'.

The final report of Reading University has, however, shown that the property market has become more flexible with a continuing trend towards shorter
leases and break clauses. A summary of the finding set out in the final report
is set out at the end of this note. The government have asked the property
industry to undertake a joint review of the Code and provide an effective
mechanism for dealing with complaints. The government also want to make
sure that everyone negotiating a lease adopts the Code, and to this end they

will be inviting the property industry to join with them in practical steps to improve the knowledge of property matters by small businesses.

On 20 April 2005 the British Property Federation issued a press release incorporating a declaration by 20 of the largest property owners in the United Kingdom in respect of an initiative being taken by them on subletting. In the future all new leases granted by these owners will permit sublettings at the market rent rather than at the higher of the passing rent and the market rent. Furthermore in respect of existing leases the declaration states that, save in five exceptional circumstances, they will waive a provision requiring sublettings to be the higher of the passing rent and the market rent. It is the expressed wish of these property owners that their initiative in these two respects will become standard policy for the commercial property industry, and they call upon all other owners and investors to follow suit.

Summary of the findings of Reading University on the Code

Earlier this year Reading University produced a report monitoring the first two years of the operation of the Code providing an independent view on whether lease structures were becoming more flexible, the extent to which tenants were now being offered a choice of alternative terms and whether or not the Code was influencing the market. The report's main findings are as follows:

Flexibility in lease terms

There has been a continuing reduction in the number of leases of over 15 years, and an increase in shorter leases of five years or less. In consequence there has been a continuing fall in the average lease length. The average length fell by two years from just under ten years in 1997 to just under eight years in 2003, the fall in lease length being more marked in office and industrial property than in the retail sector. The introduction of stamp duty land tax is thought to be an influence towards shorter leases, as also for the future is the prospect of lease accounting changes which will involve the capitalisation of lease liabilities in tenants' accounts.

The incidence of tenants' breaks has increased significantly over the Code monitoring period, and are now unlikely to be subject to stringent preconditions. Breaks are most prevalent in leases of office premises and least prevalent in retail.

Repairing liabilities, while not shifting from tenant to landlord, are now more likely to be mitigated by schedules of condition in the case of second-hand property.

Assignments and sublettings are still subject to absolute conditions; in particular, automatic authorised guarantee agreements remain standard on assignment, and subletting at no less than the rent passing under the head lease is still included in many leases.

Choice

Tenants suggest that lease length is the most frequently negotiated lease term. This was followed by break clauses, repairing liabilities, rent review interval and rent. Apart from contracting out of the 1954 Act, the type of rent review was the term least often negotiated.

Rent review

Among leases still containing rent review provisions, the upward only review is virtually universal and the incidence of alternative review types is still rare.

Review patterns remain the same with five-yearly reviews standard in the institutional market, while three-yearly reviews are still common in secondary and tertiary property on shorter leases.

The studies reveal a perception by most tenants and property agents that landlords would be unwilling to agree an up/down review, although some believe that such an alternative would be available at a price. Given the tenants' belief that rents will not fall, they are generally not prepared to pay extra rent or any other payment for the relaxation of this term.

Contracting out of the 1954 Act

The research quite clearly shows that the increase in contracting out has been dramatic and sustained. There is evidence that contracting out could be as high as 40% of new leases, although in the case of retail it is more likely to be nearer 20%. A possible explanation for this might be the unwillingness of landlords, when forced by market conditions to grant leases on less favourable terms, to risk the perpetuation of these through the process of statutory renewal. There is anecdotal evidence that the pressure on landlords to provide more flexibility for tenants is producing a desire in landlords to have their own flexibility at the end of a lease to choose whether to offer the tenant a lease renewal or to regain possession.

Report's conclusion

Overall, the picture is one of improving flexibility: reducing lease length, more tenants' breaks, reducing periods to first break, more leases without any rent review and the increased use of schedules of condition combined to give tenants more flexible arrangements. However, the Report finds the movement towards greater flexibility is not occurring in clauses relating to assignment and subletting and the type of rent review.

Recommended further reading

The author would also strongly recommend that practitioners familiarise themselves with a number of other excellent pieces of work and commentary on various aspects of commercial lease negotiation.

The first is *Service Charges in Commercial Property*, a new RICS Code of Practice (which supersedes the previous guide) and which comes into effect on1 April 2007. This Code sets out 'best practice' guidance and is intended to give guidance to practitioners as to what is expected when interpreting service charge clauses. The Code can be found on the RICS website at www.servicechargecode.co.uk. In addition, the Loughborough University Enterprises study into service charge was published on 30 November 2006.

Two recommendations are of particular interest. First, the study recommends that a combined Law Society and RICS initiative on model service charge clauses in both new and renewed leases be adopted. Secondly, the study recommends that the RICS should determine a process for implementing the new Code on both existing leases and lease renewals where otherwise it may be many years before those leases reflect the requirements of the Code.

The second publication which the author urges practitioners to look at (especially landlords' solicitors when looking for examples of draft lease clauses) is the *British Property Federation and the British Council for Offices Model Clauses* (February 2003) which has numerous excellent draft clauses and commentary on those clauses. Again, a copy of this can be found on the Internet at *www.bpf.org.uk/publications/modelclauses.html.*

A Code of Practice for Commercial Leases in England and Wales (second edition)

Published by, and reproduced here with the permission of, the Commercial Leases Working Group, 2002.

This updated Code and Explanatory Guide has been produced, at the request of the Department for Transport, Local Government and the Regions, by the Commercial Leases Working Group comprising the Association of British Insurers, Association of Property Bankers, British Retail Consortium, British Property Federation, Confederation of British Industry, Forum of Private Business, Law Society, National Association of Corporate Real Estate Executives (UK chapter), Property Market Reform Group, Royal Institution of Chartered Surveyors and Small Business Bureau. In addition, this Code has received support from the British Council for Offices, the British Chambers of Commerce, Council for Licensed Conveyancers and the Federation of Small Businesses.

This Code replaces the First Edition produced by the Commercial Leases Group in December 1995.

INTRODUCTION

This updated Code contains recommendations for landlords and tenants when they negotiate new leases of business premises and where they deal with each other during the term of a lease. The Code consists of twenty-three recommendations which an industry-wide working party, including landlord and tenant representatives, consider reflect current 'best practice' for landlords and tenants negotiating a business tenancy.

Explanatory guidance notes, set out on pages [xxi–xxx], provide the background to each of the recommendations.

Landlords and tenants should have regard to the recommendations of this Code when they negotiate lease renewals. Under current legislation if a court has to fix terms for a new lease it may decide not to change the terms from those in the existing lease.

NEGOTIATING A BUSINESS TENANCY (LEASE)

- **Recommendation 1; Renting premises:**

Both landlords and tenants should negotiate the terms of a lease openly, constructively and considering each other's views.

- **Recommendation 2; Obtaining professional advice:**

Parties intending to enter into leases should seek early advice from property professionals or lawyers.

- **Recommendation 3; Financial matters:**

Landlords should provide estimates of any service charges and other outgoings in addition to the rent. Parties should be open about their financial standing to each other, on the understanding that information provided will be kept confidential unless already publicly available or there is proper need for disclosure. The terms on which any cash deposit is to be held should be agreed and documented.

- **Recommendation 4; Duration of lease:**

Landlords should consider offering tenants a choice of length of term, including break clauses where appropriate and with or without the protection of the Landlord and Tenant Act 1954. Those funding property should make every effort to avoid imposing restrictions on the length of lease that landlords, developers and/or investors may offer.

- **Recommendation 5; Rent and value added tax:**

Where alternative lease terms are offered, different rents should be appropriately priced for each set of terms. The landlord should disclose the VAT status of the property and the tenant should take professional advice as to whether any VAT charged on rent and other charges is recoverable.

- **Recommendation 6; Rent review:**

The basis of rent review should generally be to open market rent. Wherever possible, landlords should offer alternatives which are priced on a risk-adjusted basis, including alternatives to upwards only rent reviews; these might include up/down reviews to open market rent with a minimum of the initial rent, or another basis such as annual indexation. Those funding property should make every effort to avoid imposing restrictions on the type of rent review that landlords, developers and/or investors may offer.

- **Recommendation 7; Repairs and services:**

The tenant's repairing obligations, and any repair costs included in service charges, should be appropriate to the length of the term and the condition and age of the property at the start of the lease. Where appropriate the landlord should consider appropriately priced alternatives to full repairing terms.

- **Recommendation 8; Insurance:**

Where the landlord is responsible for insuring the property, the policy terms should be competitive. The tenant of an entire building should, in appropriate cases, be given the opportunity to influence the choice of insurer. If the premises are so damaged by an uninsured risk as to prevent occupation, the tenant should be allowed to terminate the lease unless the landlord agrees to rebuild at his own cost.

- **Recommendation 9; Assigning and subletting:**

Unless the particular circumstances of the letting justify greater control, the only restriction on assignment of the whole premises should be obtaining the landlord's consent which is not to be unreasonably withheld. Landlords are urged to consider requiring Authorised Guarantee Agreements only where the assignee is of lower financial standing than the assignor at the date of the assignment.

- **Recommendation 10; Alterations and changes of use:**

Landlord's control over alterations and changes of use should not be more restrictive than is necessary to protect the value of the premises and any adjoining or neighbouring premises of the landlord. At the end of the lease the tenant should not be required to remove and make good permitted alterations unless this is reasonably required.

CONDUCT DURING A LEASE

- **Recommendation 11; Ongoing relationship:**

Landlords and tenants should deal with each other constructively, courteously, openly and honestly throughout the term of the lease and carry out their respective obligations fully and on time. If either party faces a difficulty in carrying out any obligations under the lease, the other should be told without undue delay so that the possibility of agreement on how to deal with the problem may be explored. When either party proposes to take any action which is likely to have significant consequences for the other, the party proposing the action, when it becomes appropriate to do so, should notify the other without undue delay.

- **Recommendation 12; Request for consents:**

When seeking a consent from the landlord, the tenant should supply full information about his/her proposal. The landlord should respond without undue delay and should where practicable give the tenant an estimate of the costs that the tenant will have to pay. The landlord should ensure that the request is passed promptly to any superior landlord or mortgagee whose agreement is needed and should give details to the tenant so that any problems can be speedily resolved.

- **Recommendation 13; Rent review negotiation:**

Landlords and tenants should ensure that they understand the basis upon which rent may be reviewed and the procedure to be followed, including the existence of any strict time limits which could create pitfalls. They should obtain professional advice on these matters well before the review date and also immediately upon receiving (and before responding to) any notice or correspondence on the matter from the other party or his/her agent.

- **Recommendation 14; Insurance:**

Where the landlord has arranged insurance, the terms should be made known to the tenant and any interest of the tenant covered by the policy. Any material change in the insurance should be notified to the tenant. Tenants should consider taking out their own insurance against loss or damage to contents and their business (loss of profits etc.) and any other risks not covered by the landlord's policy.

- **Recommendation 15; Varying the lease – effect on guarantors:**

Landlords and tenants should seek the agreement of any guarantors to proposed material changes to the terms of the lease, or even minor changes which could increase the guarantor's liability.

- **Recommendation 16; Holding former tenants and their guarantors liable:**

When previous tenants or their guarantors are liable to a landlord for defaults by the current tenant, landlords should notify them before the current tenant accumulates excessive liabilities. All defaults should be handled with speed and landlords should seek to assist the tenant and guarantor in minimising losses. An assignor who wishes to remain informed of the outcome of rent reviews should keep in touch with the landlord and the landlord should provide the information. Assignors should take professional advice on what methods are open to them to minimise their losses caused by defaults by the current occupier.

- **Recommendation 17; Release of landlord on sale of property:**

Landlords who sell their interest in premises should take legal advice about ending their ongoing liability under the relevant leases.

- **Recommendation 18; Repairs:**

Tenants should take the advice of a property professional about their repairing obligations near the end of the term of the lease and also immediately upon receiving a notice to repair or a schedule of dilapidations.

- **Recommendation 19; Business Rates:**

Tenants or other ratepayers should consider if their business rates assessment is correct or whether they need to make an appeal. They should refer to the DTLR Business Rates – a Guide or obtain advice from a rating specialist. The RICS provides a free rating help line service (see below) and advice is available also from the Institute of Revenues Rating and Valuation (IRRV).

- **Recommendation 20; Service charges:**

Landlords should observe the Guide to Good Practice on Service Charges in Commercial Properties. Tenants should familiarise themselves with that Guide and should take professional advice if they think they are being asked to pay excessive service charges.

- **Recommendation 21; Dispute resolution:**

When disputes arise, the parties should make prompt and reasonable efforts to settle them by agreement. Where disputes cannot be settled by agreement, both sides should always consider speed and economy when selecting a method of dispute resolution. Mediation may be appropriate before embarking on more formal procedures.

- **Recommendation 22; Repossession by the landlord:**

Tenants threatened with repossession or whose property has been repossessed will need professional advice if they wish to try to keep or regain possession. Similarly, landlords should be clear about their rights before attempting to operate a forfeiture clause and may need professional advice.

- **Recommendation 23; Renewals under the Landlord and Tenant Act 1954:**

The parties should take professional advice on the Landlord and Tenant Act 1954 and the PACT (Professional Arbitration on Court Terms) scheme at least six months before the end of the term of the lease and also immediately upon receiving any notice under the Act from the other party or their agent. Guidance on the Act can be found in the Department for Transport, Local Government and the Region's 'Guide to the Landlord and Tenant Act 1954'.

CODE OF PRACTICE – EXPLANATORY GUIDE

The Code of Practice for Commercial Leases consists of the Recommendations set out in this Guide. This Guide gives a brief explanation of the background to the recommendations. Further sources of advice and explanation are listed at the end.

NEGOTIATING A BUSINESS TENANCY (LEASE)

- **Renting premises**

Roughly a third of business premises in the UK are occupied by rent-paying tenants holding a lease (also called a 'tenancy') of the premises. Tenants should choose premises suitable for their short to medium term business plans, in respect of size, location, property and the terms of the lease. Premises might be rented, depending on the individual circumstances, either by the owner granting a new lease, by an existing tenant assigning the lease or by an existing tenant granting a sublease. The terms of a lease should reflect the type, location and condition of the property, the needs and status of the parties, and the state of the property market. All the terms in a commercial lease are normally negotiable.

For business reasons, the landlord or the tenant may wish to keep the details of their transaction confidential, but parties should avoid unnecessary secrecy. This will help the availability of market data.

Recommendation 1: Both landlords and tenants should negotiate the terms of a lease openly, constructively and considering each other's views.

- **Obtaining professional advice**

Unless landlords and tenants are fully experienced in these matters they will benefit from the advice of professional property advisers. Each party should be separately advised by independent advisers as the same person should not advise both parties. Tenants should not place reliance on advice offered by a letting agent acting for the landlord.

The main recognised property professionals are chartered surveyors regulated by the Royal Institution of Chartered Surveyors (RICS) and solicitors regulated by the Law Society and Licensed Conveyancers regulated by the Council for Licensed Conveyancers.

A surveyor can conduct, or assist in, the negotiations and can advise on the terms, including the appropriate level of rent taking into account the other terms of the letting, the location, size and quality of the property, the state of the property market, the level of business rates and other outgoings, and other relevant matters. A building surveyor can advise about the present condition of the property and about any necessary repairs. For lettings of part of a building, this can include advice about the need for major repairs and renewals of the structure or common parts which might increase service charges. A solicitor can negotiate the detailed text of the lease once the main terms have been agreed. Lease documents often run to many pages and there are no standard forms of lease. A solicitor can also check important matters such as town planning and the landlord's ownership of the property.

Recommendation 2: Parties intending to enter into leases should seek early advice from property professionals or lawyers.

- **Financial matters**

The tenant should find out about the total cost of occupying the premises – rent, service charges, insurance, business rates, utility costs etc – and ensure that they can be afforded within the budget of the business.

As the landlord will wish to assess the tenant's ability to pay those costs, particularly the rent and any service charge, the tenant should provide written references from accountants, trade suppliers and any previous landlord. If the tenant is a limited company, the landlord may also wish to see audited accounts for the last few years' trading. If this information does not exist or fails to show that the tenant has an adequate financial standing, the landlord may refuse to accept that tenant or may require guarantees from financially viable guarantors, covering not only the rent but also all other liabilities under the lease.

The landlord may also require a cash deposit, frequently of three or six months' rent. This 'rent deposit' will generally be required as security for service charges and the cost of remedying disrepair or other defaults as well as rent. There should be a proper written agreement covering the amount deposited, whether it can vary, who can hold it, how and when it can be paid over to the landlord or returned to the tenant and which party will receive any interest accruing.

The drawing up of commercial leases involves legal costs. The question of payment is a matter for negotiation between the parties. The Costs of Leases Act 1958 provides that, in the absence of agreement, each side pays its own costs.

Recommendation 3: Landlords should provide estimates of any service charges and other outgoings in addition to the rent. Parties should be open about their financial standing to each other, on the understanding that information provided will be kept confidential unless already publicly available or there is proper need for disclosure. The terms on which any cash deposit is to be held should be agreed and documented.

- **Duration of lease**

The length of the letting is called the 'term'. Leases are commonly granted for three, five, ten or fifteen year terms, but can be for terms of twenty or twenty-five years or more. A lease carries the protection of the Landlord and Tenant Act 1954, unless the parties agree to its exclusion. If the tenant occupies all or part of the premises when the lease ends, the Act enables a tenant to ask the county court to order the landlord to grant a new lease at a market rent. The landlord can refuse to grant a new lease in certain circumstances set out in the Act, for example if the tenant has seriously defaulted under the lease, or if the property is to be redeveloped or used for the landlord's own business. The tenant can ask the county court to examine the landlord's refusal to grant a new lease. In some cases, the tenant may be entitled to be paid compensation if a new lease is refused. If the lease excludes the Act, the tenant will not have the right to seek a new lease through the courts when the term expires.

Leases can contain a provision (break clause) allowing either the landlord or the tenant (or both) to terminate the lease at a specified date without waiting for the term to expire. This may be advantageous to the party who wishes to end the lease early – such as a tenant who wants to vacate without finding an assignee or subtenant, or a landlord who wants to redevelop – but early termination may cause problems and/or loss to the other party.

Recommendation 4: Landlords should consider offering tenants a choice of length of term, including break clauses where appropriate and with or without the protection of the Landlord and Tenant Act 1954. Those funding property should make every effort to avoid imposing restrictions on the length of lease that landlords, developers and/or investors may offer.

- **Rent and value added tax**

The appropriate level of rent will depend upon the state of the property market, the location, type, age, size, character and condition of the premises and the terms on which the lease is to be granted, especially the duration of the lease and the burden of repairing obligations. Rent is usually payable by quarterly installments in advance; the usual quarter days being 25 March, 24 June, 29 September and 25 December. One quarter of the yearly rent will usually be payable on these dates. This is not invariable. In some cases, particularly for short-term lettings, monthly payments might be appropriate.

Value Added Tax (VAT) will be payable on the rent (and on service charges) if the landlord has elected to waive the building's exemption from VAT. If the landlord has not already done this, it could be done at any time during the lease unless the lease forbids it. If this waiver is made, VAT will be payable by the tenant in addition to the rent and service charge. Many tenants will be entitled to recover the VAT through their business VAT returns.

Recommendation 5: Where alternative lease terms are offered, different rents should be appropriately priced for each set of terms. The landlord should disclose the VAT status of the property and the tenant should take professional advice as to whether any VAT charged on rent and other charges is recoverable.

- **Rent review**

For leases over five years, it is usual for the rent to be reviewed at stated intervals. Usually rent is reviewed to open market rent level – the rent that a new tenant would pay if the property was being let in the open market at the time of the review (the most appropriate basis for review). Alternatives include fixed increases or linking the rent to a published index (such as the Index of Retail Prices) or to the annual turnover of the tenant's business at the premises. Reviews to open market rent normally occur every five years whilst rents linked to indices or turnover are commonly recalculated annually. Not all these methods of review are suitable for every tenant or appropriate to every type of property or business.

If the review is on 'upwards only' terms, the rent will not reduce at review but will remain at its existing level even if the market rent or index has fallen. Tenants may find that they would have to pay a higher initial rent where the rent review is to be up or down compared with upwards only, as this transfers the risk of downward movements to the landlord. Financers of property require landlords to ensure that rental income will not fall below a particular level and this may restrict a landlord's ability to agree an upwards/downwards basis.

Recommendation 6: The basis of rent review should generally be to open market rent. Wherever possible, landlords should offer alternatives which are priced on a risk-adjusted basis, including alternatives to upwards only rent reviews; these might include up/down reviews to open market rent with a minimum of the initial rent, or another basis such as annual indexation. Those funding property should make every effort to avoid imposing restrictions on the type of rent review that landlords, developers and/or investors may offer.

• **Repairs and services**

Leases generally state which party will be responsible for carrying out, or for meeting the cost of, repairing and maintaining the fabric and services of the property. The degree to which these burdens are placed on the tenant should take into account the initial condition of the premises and the duration of the lease.

A 'full repairing' lease makes the tenant of an entire building responsible for all internal and external repairs and redecoration that become necessary during the term. This includes the roof, foundations, main walls and other structural parts, irrespective of whether or not they are in good condition at the start of the lease. A 'full repairing' lease for part of a building requires the tenant to maintain and decorate the inside of the premises and to pay, through a service charge, towards the landlord's costs of maintaining and repairing the common parts and structure and providing services such as porterage, lifts, central heating, etc. Such obligations might require the tenant to carry out, or pay towards the cost of, work to remedy an inherent construction defect which becomes apparent during the term.

Alternatives to 'full repairing' terms might include limiting the tenant's repairs to the maintenance of the property in its existing condition, excluding certain categories of repair, and the remediation of inherent defects. The scope or amount of any service charge can be limited or there can be a fixed rent which is inclusive of service costs. If the lease refers to the existing condition of the property, it will be in both parties' interests for a schedule of condition (which can be photographic) to be professionally prepared and kept with the lease documents.

Professional advice should be sought when the tenant is required to carry out initial improvements and repairs, as there may be implications for tax and rent review.

Recommendation 7: The tenant's repairing obligations, and any repair costs included in service charges, should be appropriate to the length of the term and the condition and age of the property at the start of the lease. Where appropriate the landlord should consider appropriately priced alternatives to full repairing terms.

• Insurance

It is usual for the landlord to insure the building and require the tenants to pay the premiums. In the case of multi-occupied buildings, each tenant would be expected to contribute towards the total insurance premium; this may be included in the service charge or may be charged separately. Leases may give the landlord discretion to choose the insurer. Alternatives include allowing the tenant to influence the selection of the insurer (if their lease covers the entire building), or providing that the landlord must arrange the insurance on competitive rates.

The lease should contain provisions covering the situation where there is damage by an uninsured risk or where there is a large excess. These risks vary from time to time and might include terrorist damage. If suitable provisions are not included in the lease the tenant might have to meet the cost of rebuilding in that situation. Alternatives include allowing the tenant to terminate the lease following uninsured damage, although it may be appropriate to allow the landlord to choose to rebuild at his own cost in order to keep the lease in force.

Recommendation 8: Where the landlord is responsible for insuring the property, the policy terms should be competitive. The tenant of an entire building should, in appropriate cases, be given the opportunity to influence the choice of insurer. If the premises are so damaged by an uninsured risk as to prevent occupation, the tenant should be allowed to terminate the lease unless the landlord agrees to rebuild at his own cost.

• Assigning and subletting

There are two ways in which the tenant may pass on the lease obligations to a third party; one is by assignment (selling, giving away or paying someone to take over, the lease) and the other is by subletting (remaining as tenant of the lease with the lease obligations but granting a sublease to another tenant who undertakes the same or similar obligations). Leases generally control assignment and subletting. Most require the tenant to obtain the landlord's consent (which cannot be unreasonably withheld) but some leases completely prohibit certain acts such as subletting part of the premises. A new lease, and an existing lease granted since 1995, may expand the landlord's right to control assignments by imposing credit ratings or other financial criteria for assignees. It may also require the assigning tenant to stand as guarantor for any assignee by giving the landlord an 'Authorised Guarantee Agreement'; alternatives include giving this guarantee only if it is reasonably required by the landlord, such as where the assignee is of lower financial standing than the assigning tenant.

Recommendation 9: Unless the particular circumstances of the letting justify greater control, the only restriction on assignment of the whole premises should be obtaining the landlord's consent which is not to be unreasonably withheld. Landlords are urged to consider requiring Authorised Guarantee Agreements only where the assignee is of lower financial standing than the assignor at the date of the assignment.

• Alterations and changes of use

Leases generally restrict the tenant's freedom to make alterations and often impose tighter control over external and structural alterations than over internal non-structural alterations or partitioning. The lease may absolutely prohibit the work. Alternatives may require the landlord's consent which must not be unreasonably withheld, or may permit the particular type of alteration without consent. The lease may entitle the landlord to require the tenant to reinstate the premises (remove alterations) at the end of the lease; or alternatively reinstatement need only take place if it is reasonable for the landlord to require it.

The permitted use of the premises may be very narrowly defined or there may be a wide class of use. Consent for changes of use can be at the landlord's discretion or, alternatively, the lease may provide that consent is not to be unreasonably withheld. If the provisions of the lease are very restrictive this can hinder the assignment of the lease or the subletting of the property to a different business.

Recommendation 10: Landlord's control over alterations and changes of use should not be more restrictive than is necessary to protect the value of the premises and any adjoining or neighbouring premises of the landlord. At the end of the lease the tenant should not be required to remove and make good permitted alterations unless this is reasonably required.

CONDUCT DURING A LEASE

• Ongoing relationship

The relationship between landlord and tenant will continue after the lease has been signed; for example, there may be rent review negotiations or discussions about varying the terms. The landlord may be contemplating planning applications, redevelopment, improvements or making changes in the provision of services.

Recommendation 11: Landlords and tenants should deal with each other constructively, courteously, openly and honestly throughout the term of the lease and carry out their respective obligations fully and on time. If either party faces a difficulty in carrying out any obligations under the lease, the other should be told without undue delay so that the possibility of agreement on how to deal with the problem may be explored. When either party proposes to take any action which is likely to have significant consequences for the other, the party proposing the action, when it becomes appropriate to do so, should notify the other without undue delay.

- **Request for consents**

There may be occasions when the tenant seeks a consent (licence) from the landlord, when for example, the tenant proposes to assign the lease, grant a sublease, change the use of the property, make alterations or display signs. The effect on the landlord will vary with the exact details. In some cases, the landlord will have to pass the request to a superior landlord or to a mortgagee. Most leases require the tenant to pay any costs incurred by the landlord in dealing with such an application.

Recommendation 12: When seeking a consent from the landlord, the tenant should supply full information about his/her proposal. The landlord should respond without undue delay and should where practicable give the tenant an estimate of the costs that the tenant will have to pay. The landlord should ensure that the request is passed promptly to any superior landlord or mortgagee whose agreement is needed and should give details to the tenant so that any problems can be speedily resolved.

- **Rent review negotiation**

Many leases contain provisions for the periodic review of rent; these may be highly technical and may lay down procedures and time limits.

Recommendation 13: Landlords and tenants should ensure that they understand the basis upon which rent may be reviewed and the procedure to be followed, including the existence of any strict time limits which could create pitfalls. They should obtain professional advice on these matters well before the review date and also immediately upon receiving (and before responding to) any notice or correspondence on the matter from the other party or his/her agent.

- **Insurance**

Directly or indirectly, the tenant will usually pay the cost of insuring the premises and the lease will state whether the tenant or the landlord has to arrange this. Where the landlord has arranged insurance, the terms should be made known to the tenant and any interest of the tenant covered by the policy.

Sometimes the lease allows the landlord or the tenant to end the lease if the premises are very badly damaged. If damage occurs but is covered by the insurance, there may be important questions about how, why and by whom the insurance money is spent and the parties should take professional advice as soon as the damage occurs.

Recommendation 14: Where the landlord has arranged insurance, the terms should be made known to the tenant and any interest of the tenant covered by the policy. Any material change in the insurance should be notified to the tenant. Tenants should consider taking out their own insurance against loss or damage to contents and their business (loss of profits etc.) and any other risks not covered by the landlord's policy.

- **Varying the lease – effect on guarantors**

A guarantor may not be liable if the terms of the lease are changed without the guarantor's consent. In some cases the variation may release a guarantor from all liability.

Recommendation 15: Landlords and tenants should seek the agreement of any guarantors to any proposed material changes to the terms of the lease, or even minor changes which could increase the guarantor's liability.

- **Holding former tenants and their guarantors liable**

A tenant who assigns a lease may remain liable for a period for any subsequent breach of the lease terms including failure to pay rent. This liability may also apply to a guarantor for the former tenant. Where payment is made to the landlord under this liability, the former tenant may be entitled to take an overriding lease of the property in order to have some control over the current tenants; legal advice can be obtained about these matters. In certain circumstances, insurance against losses following an assignment may be possible. Landlords must notify previous tenants about arrears of rent and service charges within six months of the amount becoming due, in order to make them liable.

Recommendation 16: When previous tenants or their guarantors are liable to a landlord for defaults by the current tenant, landlords should notify them before the current tenant accumulates excessive liabilities. All defaults should be handled with speed and landlords should seek to assist the tenant and guarantor in minimising losses. An assignor who wishes to remain informed of the outcome of rent reviews should keep in touch with the landlord and the landlord should provide the information. Assignors should take professional advice on what methods are open to them to minimise their losses caused by defaults by the current occupier.

- **Release of landlord on sale of property**

A landlord who sells his interest in the building may remain liable to the tenants to perform any obligations in the lease (for example, in repairing or insuring the building) in the event of failure on the part of the new landlord. It is possible, in certain circumstances, for landlords to terminate their obligations on selling the property through provisions in the lease or, in some cases by seeking the agreement of their tenants and, in the event of objection, decision by a county court.

Recommendation 17: Landlords who sell their interest in premises should take legal advice about ending their ongoing liability under the lease.

- **Repairs**

The landlord may be entitled to serve a notice requiring the tenant to undertake repairing obligations which the tenant has failed to carry out. This notice may be served near or at the end of the term or earlier. The list of repairs is called a 'schedule of dilapidations'. Disagreements about these are not uncommon and the law on repairing obligations is complex.

Recommendation 18: Tenants should take the advice of a property professional about their repairing obligations near the end of the term of the lease and also immediately upon receiving a notice to repair or a schedule of dilapidations.

- **Business Rates**

Uniform Business Rates (UBR) are payable to local authorities and are the responsibility of the occupier (the ratepayer) of the property. In certain circumstances the amount payable can be reduced by appealing against the business rates assessment. Ratepayers should be aware that time limits apply to certain appeal procedures and advice on these may be obtained from a rating specialist, who is usually a chartered surveyor.

Recommendation 19: Tenants or other ratepayers should consider if their business rates assessment is correct or whether they need to make an appeal. They should refer to the DTLR Business Rates – a Guide or obtain advice from a rating specialist. RICS provides a free rating help line service and advice is available also from the Institute of Revenues Rating and Valuation (IRRV).

- **Service charges**

Where the lease entitles the landlord to levy a service charge, details of the services covered are usually set out in the lease and it may contain provisions requiring the landlord to act reasonably or economically. Some leases lay down strict time limits for the tenant to query service charges. Several leading property industry and professional bodies have agreed a Guide to Good Practice in relation to service charges which is available free.

Recommendation 20: Landlords should observe the Guide to Good Practice on Service Charges in Commercial Properties. Tenants should familiarise themselves with that Guide and should take professional advice if they think they are being asked to pay excessive service charges.

• Dispute resolution

Disputes between landlords and tenants can be expensive, time-consuming and divisive. If the lease does not state how a particular dispute is to be settled, the parties may have to go to court. Leases often provide for certain types of dispute to be resolved by particular procedures; for example, it is common to provide that a dispute about rent review is to be referred to an independent surveyor acting either as an arbitrator or as an expert. Professional advice should be obtained about any procedures laid down in the lease.

The parties can agree to appoint a mediator to try to resolve a particular dispute even though the lease does not provide for it. The mediator will consult both parties separately and advise them on the strengths or weaknesses of their case and work towards a settlement. Mediators should be able to keep costs down and achieve an outcome within a short timescale; but if mediation fails, delay and cost will have been incurred and the parties still have to resort to the formal procedures of arbitration, expert determination or court proceedings.

Recommendation 21: When disputes arise, the parties should make prompt and reasonable efforts to settle them by agreement. Where disputes cannot be settled by agreement, both sides should always consider speed and economy when selecting a method of dispute resolution. Mediation may be appropriate before embarking on more formal procedures.

• Repossession by the landlord

The lease will contain a clause giving the landlord the right ('forfeiture' or 're-entry') to repossess the property if the tenant breaks any obligations under the lease or becomes insolvent. When a landlord seeks repossession under a forfeiture clause, the tenant (or sub-tenant) may be entitled to claim 'relief from forfeiture' from a court, i.e. the right to retain the property despite the breach.

Recommendation 22: Tenants threatened with repossession or whose property has been repossessed will need professional advice if they wish to try to keep or regain possession. Similarly, landlords should be clear about their rights before attempting to operate a forfeiture clause and may need professional advice.

- **Renewals under the Landlord and Tenant Act 1954**

Unless it is excluded, this Act may give the tenant a right to renew the lease when it ends (see under Duration of lease). It contains procedures and time limits that must be strictly followed by both landlords and tenants. Disputes under the Act about whether the tenant should be granted a new lease and about its terms are adjudicated by the county court, but the parties may agree to ask the court to refer all or some aspects to be decided by an independent surveyor or solicitor under the Professional Arbitration on Court Terms scheme operated by the RICS and the Law Society.

Recommendation 23: The parties should take professional advice on the Landlord and Tenant Act 1954 and the PACT scheme at least six months before the end of the term of the lease and also immediately upon receiving any notice under the Act from the other party or their agent. Guidance on the Act can be found in the Department for Transport, Local Government and the Regions, 'Guide to the Landlord and Tenant Act 1954'.

DATE [   ] 20[   ]

1. [   ]

2. [   ]

3. [   ]

LEASE

relating to

[   ]

INDEX

PRESCRIBED INFORMATION

Clauses Prescribed by Land Registration Rules 2003

LR1   Date of lease

LR2   Title number(s)

LR2.1   Landlord's title number(s)

Title number(s) out of which this lease is granted. Leave blank if not registered

LR2.2   Other title matters

Existing title number(s) against which entries of matters referred to in LR9, LR10, LR11 and LR13 are to be made

LR3   Parties to this lease

Give full names, addresses and company's registration number, if any, of each of the parties. For Scottish companies use a SC prefix and for limited liability partnerships use an OC prefix. For foreign companies give territory in which incorporated

Landlord

Tenant

Other parties

Specify capacity of each party, for example, 'management company', 'guarantor', etc

LR4   Property

Insert a full description of the land being leased

Or

Refer to the clause, schedule or paragraph of a schedule in this lease in which the land being leased is more fully described

Where there is a letting of part of a registered title, a plan must be attached to this lease and any floor levels must be specified

In the case of a conflict between this clause and the remainder of this lease then, for the purposes of registration, this clause shall prevail.

COMMENTARY

Prescribed information

A major change in Land Registry practice will take effect on 19 June 2006. A lease that is granted out of a registered title that needs to be registered will have to contain fourteen prescribed and appropriately completed clauses by virtue of Part 2 of the Land Registration (Amendment) (No 2) Rules 2005, which are as follows:

(1) Date of lease

(2) Title number(s)

(3) Parties to the lease

(4) Property

(5) Prescribed statement (affecting charities and certain residential leases)

(6) Term

(7) Premium, inclusive of VAT

(8) Prohibition/restrictions on disposal

(9) Rights of acquisition that need to be noted on the register – three categories of option – namely an option to renew or acquire the reversion, tenant's covenant to (or offer to) surrender and any landlord's contractual right to acquire the lease

(10) Restrictive covenants by the landlord in respect of land other than the demised property

(11) Easements by cross reference to clauses in the lease

(12) Application for a standard form of restriction

(13) Estate rent charge again by cross reference

(14) Declaration of trust where more than one person comprises the tenant.

The information set out above is what the Land Registry regard as essential for registration purposes. The benefit of this to tenants is that the completion of the prescribed clauses will provide protection on the register of all ancillary rights granted in the lease, for example, easements and options.

For those leases that the Land Registry received between 9 January 2006 and 18 June 2006 the new rules were in force which meant that the prescribed clauses could have been used but were not mandatory. The clauses must appear at the front of the lease or immediately after any front sheet and index/contents page. Any 'Particulars' page will therefore have to be included after the prescribed clauses.

The insertion of the prescribed information is not compulsory for leases granted out of an unregistered title whatever the length of the term, but, it is suggested, that it is likely to become good practice to include this in all leases as a sensible way of setting out at the front of the lease important information for both the original parties and their successors in title.

LR5   **Prescribed statements etc**

If this lease includes a statement falling within LR5.1, insert under that sub-clause the relevant statement or refer to the clause, schedule or paragraph of a schedule in this lease which contained the statement

In LR5.2, omit or delete those Acts which do not apply to this lease

LR5.1   **Statements prescribed under rules 179 (dispositions in favour of a charity), 180 (dispositions by a charity) or 196 (leases under the Leasehold Reform, Housing and Urban Development Act 1993) of the Land Registration Rules 2003**

LR5.2   **This lease is made under, or by reference to, provisions of:**

Leasehold Reform Act 1967

Housing Act 1985

Housing Act 1988

Housing Act 1996

LR6   **Term for which the Property is leased**

Include only the appropriate statement (duly completed) from the three options

NOTE: The information you provide, or refer to here, will be used as part of the particulars to identify the lease under rule 6 of the Land Registration Rules 2003.

From and including

To and including

OR

The term as specified in this lease at clause/schedule/paragraph

OR

The term is as follows:

LR7   **Premium**

Specify the total premium, inclusive of any VAT where payable

LR8   **Prohibitions or restrictions on disposing of this lease**

Include whichever of the two statements is appropriate

Do not set out here the wording of the provision

This lease does not contain a provision that prohibits or restricts dispositions

LR9   **Rights of acquisition etc**

Insert the relevant provisions in the sub-clauses or refer to the clause, schedule or paragraph of a schedule in this lease which contains the provisions

LR9.1   **Tenant's contractual rights to renew this lease, to acquire the reversion or another lease of the Property, or to acquire an interest in other land**

L9.2   **Tenant's covenant to (or offer to) surrender this lease**

L9.3   **Landlord's contractual rights to acquire this lease**

LR10   **Restrictive covenants given in this lease by the Landlord in respect of land other than the Property**

Insert the relevant provisions or reefer to the clause, schedule or paragraph of a schedule in this lease which contains the provisions

LR11   **Easements**

Refer here only to the clause, schedule or paragraph of a schedule in this lease which sets out the easements

LR11.1   **Easements granted by this lease for the benefit of the Property**

LR11.2   **Easements granted or reserved by this lease over the Property for the benefit of other property**

LR12   **Estate rentcharge burdening the Property**

Refer here only to the clause, schedule or paragraph of a schedule in this lease which sets out the rentcharge

LR13   **Application for standard form of restriction**

Set out the full text of the standard form of restriction and the title against which it is to be entered. If you wish to apply for

more than one standard form of restriction use this clause to apply for each other them, tell us who is applying against which title and set out the full text of the restriction you are applying for

Standard forms of restriction are set out in Schedule 4 to the Land Registration Rules 2003

The Parties to this lease apply to enter the following standard form of restriction [against the title of the Property] or [against title number]

LR14   Declaration of trust where there is more than one person comprising the Tenant

If the Tenant is one person, omit or delete all the alternative statements

If the Tenant is more than one person, complete this clause by omitting or deleting all inapplicable alternative statements

The Tenant is more than one person. They are to hold the Property on trust for themselves as joint tenants

OR

The Tenant is more than one person. They are to hold the Property on trust for themselves as tenants in common in equal shares

OR

The Tenant is more than one person. They are to hold the Property on trust Complete as necessary

DATE   20[   ]

PARTIES

1   *'Landlord'*   [   ] of [   ]
                              whose   registered   office   is   at
                              [   ] (Registered in
                              England: Company Registration Number:
                              [   ])

2   *'Original Tenant'*   [   ] of [   ]
                              whose   registered   office   is   at
                              [   ] (Registered in
                              England: Company Registration Number:
                              [   ])

3   *'Guarantor'*   [   ] of [   ]
                              [whose   registered   office   is   at
                              [   ]   Company
                              Registration Number [   ]

OPERATIVE PROVISIONS

1   **DEFINITIONS AND INTERPRETATION**

          For all purposes of this Lease (unless the context otherwise
          requires) the terms defined in this clause have the meanings
          specified

1.1   *'Accountant'*   [   ] or any other person who
                              may be an employee of the Landlord or a
                              Group Company but any person so
                              appointed to act as an Accountant must
                              be an Associate or Fellow of the Institute
                              of Chartered Accountants in England and
                              Wales

PARTIES

If a company is a party to the lease (either as landlord, tenant or guarantor) it is essential that its company registration number and registered office are stated. It is important to be able to trace the relevant corporate party through what is often a maze of corporate transactions. The only certain way of doing this is to ensure company registration numbers (which are unique identity codes) are stated. The unique identification code of the company number is often used by some of the registries, eg HM Land Registry, and it also helps in making a search at Companies House. It is also essential to ensure that the company registered office is stated as this information is necessary to ensure compliance with the relevant provisions relating to service of notices, although a search at Companies House to check that it has not changed at the time of the search is obviously necessary. As a further point, if a corporate tenant is registered or stated as having an address offshore, it is good practice for an address for service in the UK to be given. A company search should reveal all relevant details.

It is essential that a guarantor is advised to take separate and independent legal advice, since there is a clear conflict of interest between a tenant and a guarantor. The advice to the guarantor may well be not to give the guarantee, which will result in the lease not being granted to the tenant. Furthermore there are likely to be substantial amendments which can be made to the guarantee provisions to protect the guarantor. This applies even where a solicitor is acting for the company and is also asked, or is assumed to be acting also on behalf of the controlling directors of that company who are to act as guarantors. Have the controlling directors considered the consequences should they sell the company during the term of the lease? The company solicitor, it is suggested, should decline to act for the directors, record that advice and confirm it in writing if they choose not to have separate legal representation. In practice however, this can lead to difficulties with clients.

OPERATIVE PROVISIONS

1   DEFINITIONS AND INTERPRETATION

1.1   Any professional person called upon to perform any duty or function pursuant to the terms of the lease should be required to be a member of that profession's governing body, eg The Law Society, the Royal Institution of Chartered Surveyors etc. Not only will there be the requisite level of expertise but membership of such a body will ensure that any functions or duties undertaken pursuant to the terms of the lease are conducted within the ambit of the professional and ethical code laid down by that governing body. While there are various regulatory bodies for the accountancy profession, the Institute of Chartered Accountants in England and Wales is the author's preferred option.

1.2 *'Additional Parking'* the parking bays numbered [   ] to [   ] inclusive in the car park of the Building shown [for the purposes of identification only] edged brown on Plan No 1

1.3 *'Adjoining Conduits'* all the pipes, sewers, drains, mains, ducts, conduits, gutters, watercourses, wires, cables, channels, flues and all other conducting media, laser optical fibres, data or impulse transmission, communication or reception systems and includes any fixings, louvres, cowls, covers and other ancillary apparatus that are in, on or under the Building and serve the Premises

1.4 *'Adjoining property of the Landlord'* references to 'adjoining property of the Landlord' are references to each and every part of the neighbouring or adjoining land, excluding the Building, in which the Landlord or a Group Company has or during the Term acquires an interest or estate

1.5 *'Building'* all that building known as [   ] and surrounding land shown for the purpose of identification only edged black on the Plan No 1

1.6 *'Common Parts'* the areas and amenities made available from time to time by the Landlord for use in common by the tenants and occupiers of the Building and all persons expressly or by implication authorised by them including the [pedestrian ways], [forecourts], [car parks], [loading bays], [service roads], [landscaped areas], [entrance halls], [landings], [lifts], l[ift-shafts], [staircases, passages] and [areas designated for the keeping and collecting of refuse], but not limited to them PROVIDED ALWAYS that the landlord shall ensure at all times that sufficient areas of the common parts are available for use by the tenant to enable the tenant or any lawful sub-tenant or other occupier to undertake its usual business at the Premises without a detrimental effect on its business

1.2   Car parking spaces, particularly in relation to office accommoda-
       tion, can be an emotive issue for tenants and their employees. It is
       absolutely vital that any parking bays or parking areas referred to in
       the lease as being for the use of the tenant, and the extent of any
       such rights, are accurately defined. As a tenant it is infinitely prefer-
       able to have the actual car parking spaces demised rather than sim-
       ply being given a right to use them as the demise will confer
       exclusive possession of the parking bays on the tenant. The only
       downside for the tenant might be that the repairing covenant would
       extend to the car parking spaces as they form part of the demise. As
       regards reference to the plan, or any plan, it is vital to state whether
       any verbal description of the premises, building, car parking space,
       etc is to take precedence over the plan or vice versa.

1.3   This allows for the additional conduits often now required in the
       light of modern technology.

1.5   The building as defined in the lease needs to be accurately identi-
       fied by reference to a detailed plan.

1.6   It is vital that sufficient access is available to a tenant to secure use
       of the premises. The proviso added at the end of the clause achieves
       this.

1.7	*'Conduits'*	the pipes, sewers, drains, mains, ducts, conduits, gutters, watercourses, wires, cables, <u>laser optical fibres, data or impulse transmission, communication or reception systems</u>, channels, flues and all other conducting media – including any fixings, louvres, cowls, covers and any other ancillary apparatus – that are in on over or under the Premises
1.8	*'Contractual Term'*	[ ] years from <u>and including</u> the day of 20 <u>and ending at midnight on the day of 20</u>
1.9	*'Decorating Years'*	[ ]
1.10	*'Default Interest Rate'*	the rate of ~~[5]~~* [2] % per year above the Interest Rate
1.11	*'Development'*	References to 'development' are references to development as defined by the Town and Country Planning Act 1990 section 55
1.12	*'Group Company'*	a company that is a member of the same group as the Tenant within the meaning of the 1954 Act section 42
1.13	*'Guarantor'*	includes [not only the person named above as the Guarantor, but also] any person who enters into covenants with the Landlord pursuant to **clause 3.9.5.2** CONDITIONS or **clause 3.22** REPLACEMENT GUARANTOR
1.14	*~~'Headlease'~~*	<u>a lease dated [ ] and made between (1) [ ], (2) [ ] [and (3) [ ]]</u>
1.15	*'Included Parking Bays'*	the parking bays numbered [ ] to [ ] inclusive in the car park of the Building, shown coloured green on Plan <u>No 1</u>

1.7   The same comment applies as in the note to **clause 1.3**.

1.8   Due to the legal rules relating to service of notices, whether pursuant to a rent review clause, option to determine or any other provision in the lease which requires a technical interpretation of dates, it is vital that the term commencement date is not open to doubt. The amendment proposed makes quite clear the date on which the term commences and the time and date when the term ends. If a term is stated to commence 'from' a certain date the general rule of law is that, in fact, it commences at the beginning of the following day and it ends at midnight on the anniversary of the date 'from' which it is granted. Although the courts have in several cases recently relaxed the very strict rules relating to compliance with strict timetables in favour of the 'reasonable recipient' test (see *Mannai Investment Co Ltd v Eagle Star Life Assurance Co Ltd* [1997] AC 749, *HL Garston v Scottish Widows' Fund* and *Life Assurance Society* [1998] 3 All ER 596, CA and *Peer Freeholds Limited v Clean Wash International* [2005] 17 EG 124) there is absolutely no need to leave anything in doubt and risk a claim for negligence.

    Recommendation 4 of the Code: *Duration of lease: Landlords should consider offering tenants a choice of length of term, including break clauses where appropriate and with or without the protection of the Landlord and Tenant Act 1954. Those funding property should make every effort to avoid imposing restrictions on the length of lease that landlords, developers and/or investors may offer.*

1.10   For the relevance of this definition, refer to **clause 3.17** relating to the payment of interest on arrears where the tenant is in default. See also the definition of 'Interest Rate' in **clause 1.23**. It is considered that the rate of interest at 5% (as originally drafted) is too high and punitive. By amending the rate to 2% the hope is that a compromise of 3% or 4% will be agreed.

1.11   While no amendment is suggested here it would have been had the definition of *Group Company* made reference to any statutory definition contained in either the Companies Act legislation or the taxation legislation which is much more restrictive as opposed to section 42 of the Landlord and Tenant Act 1954. The Landlord and Tenant Act 1954 definition gives much more flexibility.

1.13   The words in square brackets need to be deleted if there is no guarantor of the original tenant.

1.14   References to a headlease are simply to cater for the situation where the lease being negotiated is a sub-lease rather than a headlease itself.

1.16	*'Inherent Defect'*	any defect in the Premises or the Building or in anything installed in or on the Premises or the Building which is attributable to:
	(i)	defective design;
	(ii)	defective workmanship or materials,
	(iii)	defective supervision of the construction of or the installation of anything in or on the Premises or the Building;
	(iv)	defective preparation of the site upon which the Premises or the Building are constructed.
1.17	*'Initial Provisional Service Charge'*	£[ ] per year

1.18	*'Initial Rent'*	the sum of £[ ] per year

1.16   This new definition is to be inserted in appropriate circumstances where the tenant is to have no liability for any inherent defects in the Premises or the Building of which they form part. It is vital that it is coupled with a proviso in the tenant's repairing obligation excluding the remedying of inherent defects from the tenant's covenant (see **clause 3.4.1**), and further coupling with it a new landlord's covenant to remedy any latent defects which manifest themselves in the Premises or the Building of which it forms part (see **clause 4.7**). Finally the tenant must ensure that the landlord, having remedied the inherent defect, cannot or does not attempt to recover the cost through the service charge (see Schedule 6 para 2.3.2). Clearly whether or not it is appropriate to remove the remedying of inherent defects from the tenant's covenant will depend upon the circumstances of each individual letting. The author would suggest that certainly in relation to new buildings where collateral warranties or duty of care agreements are not available in favour of the tenant, the tenant must absolutely not accept any obligation to make good inherent defects. If the landlord has failed to structure his development in such a way to obtain these collateral warranties or duty of care agreements in favour of the tenant, then the risk should not rest with the tenant.

The tenant's adviser needs to be aware of the limited scope of any duty of care which the original design and construction team owe to the tenant. The duty is exceptionally limited, firstly, to a duty to take reasonable care that the building is not a danger to health and safety and, secondly, this duty of care does not extend to pure economic loss, an example of which would be the cost of repair. Whilst the Contracts (Rights of Third Parties) Act 1999 does offer some limited protection to the tenant most leases tend to exclude the application of this Act (see **clause 8.18**) and the suggested amendments avoid any uncertainty. If, however, the landlord is not prepared to go this far, an alternative would be to seek some form of undertaking (whether by a supplemental deed or side letter) from the original developer, that the developer would pursue such remedies as he has under the original letters of appointment, or building contract agreements with the original design and construction team, and to apply any damages which are successfully recovered in making good the problems that have manifested themselves at no cost to the tenant.

1.18   Factual gaps in the draft lease must be carefully checked and completed by reference to the heads of terms agreed between the parties.

Recommendation 5 of the Code: Rent and value added tax: *Where alternative lease terms are offered, different rents should be appropriately priced for each set of terms. The landlord should disclose the VAT status of the property and the tenant should take professional advice as to whether any VAT charged on rent and other charges is recoverable.*

1.19   *'Insurance Rent'*   the Insurance Rent Percentage of the ~~gross~~ reasonable competitive sums net of any commission paid to, or discount received by, the Landlord ~~including any commission~~ that ~~Landlord is from time to time liable to pay~~ that is reasonably and properly expended or required to be expended by the Landlord:

(i)   by way of premium for insuring the Building, including insuring for loss of rent, in accordance with his obligations contained in this Lease or, where the insurance includes the Building and other property, the proportion of those sums reasonably attributable to the Building

(ii)   by way of premium for insuring in such amount and on such terms as the Landlord (acting reasonably) considers fair and proper ~~appropriate~~ against all liability of the Landlord to third parties arising out of or in connection with any matter involving or relating to the Building and

(iii)   for insurance valuations (but not more than once in any calendar year)

and all of any increased premium payable by reason of any act or omission of the Tenant or anyone at the Premises ~~with the Tenant's consent or any invitee employee or guest of the Tenant~~ and under the Tenant's control

1.19   Insurance rent payments by the tenant should be by way of indemnity only. There should be no profit element or unjust enrichment for the landlord. If the gross premium purportedly payable by the landlord for insuring the premises is netted down to take account of any discounts allowed to him or commission paid to him then, clearly if the tenant makes the full gross repayment, there is a profit element for the landlord. The tenant should forcibly resist any attempt by the landlord to profit in this way. Indeed there may be circumstances where a tenant is able to get a better deal than the landlord, eg a retailer with a larger number of shops throughout the country. The tenant should strenuously resist any profiteering by the landlord although, as will be a recurring theme throughout the commentary, the relative bargaining strengths of the parties are in practice likely to be paramount. As the law currently stands there is no term to be implied which means that any insurance premiums paid by the landlord must be reasonable (*Havenridge Ltd v Boston Dyers Ltd* [1994] 2 EGLR 73, CA and *Berrycroft Management 6 Ltd v Sinclair Gardens Investments (Kensington) Ltd* [1997] 22 EG 114) and it is vital therefore that the concept of reasonableness is introduced into both the cost of such premiums and its expenditure.

1.19(i)   The concept of reasonableness introduced here is self-explanatory and should not give the landlord cause for concern.

1.19(ii) Again, the concepts of 'reasonableness' and 'fair and proper' here should not cause the landlord a problem. If the landlord is not prepared to accept an obligation to act reasonably then the tenant can, in the author's view, validly argue that the only implication to be drawn from this is that the landlord may seek to be unreasonable and perhaps a more serious question ought to be asked by the tenant about the basis of the relationship with the landlord on which he is about to embark. Is your client tenant willing to proceed with the lease on such a footing?

1.19(iii) Initially the tenant should resist an obligation to pay for valuations although the landlord's arguments are likely to win the day here. However, the tenant should not be obliged to pay for this more than once in any calendar year. If the landlord chooses to change his insurers (or brokers) that is a decision for the landlord, and the tenant should not be penalised in cost terms for this.

          The amendment at the end of **clause 1.16** (again to be a recurring theme throughout this commentary) seeks to mitigate the harsh effects of the wide class of persons covered by this clause as originally drafted. The landlord, perhaps understandably, wants the clause to be as wide as possible but the tenant's argument is that the tenant cannot be responsible, for example, for any member of the public, or independent contractor or licensee, who happens to wander into or be on the premises who is not under his control. There should be an element of control by the tenant as there would be with an employee and the amendment to this clause achieves this.

1.20	*'Insurance Rent Percentage'*	[ ]%

1.21	*'Insured Risks'*	the risks of loss or damage by fire, storm, tempest, earthquake, lightning, explosion, <u>Terrorism</u>, riot, civil commotion, malicious damage, impact by vehicles and by aircraft and articles dropped from aircraft (other than war risks), flood damage and bursting and overflowing of water pipes and tanks and such other risks <u>whether or not in the nature of the foregoing against which a reasonably prudent landlord (acting reasonably) would normally insure, and also such other risks as a Tenant may from time to time reasonably require</u> ~~whether or not in the nature of the foregoing, as the Landlord from time to time decides to insure against~~

1.20   Although not a specifically suggested amendment, the tenant's adviser should be aware of the circumstances in which a stated percentage should be capable of being varied. Refer to Schedule 6 paragraph 2.6 which makes provision for the variation of the percentage.

1.21   The risks for the tenant in relation to this clause as originally drawn are quite clear. If damage is caused to the property by anything other than an *insured risk* then, on the basis that the lease is a full repairing and insuring one, any such uninsured damage will fall to be repaired and paid for by the tenant. The tenant should, therefore, ensure that the insured risks stated are as wide as possible and should also include a general sweeper up. Clearly each property needs to be considered on its own merits and input from a surveyor would be very advisable and, particularly if the lawyer is not familiar with the area where the subject property is located, essential. While the landlord himself has a vested interest in ensuring adequate insurance is in place, if for any reason the policy is faulty or certain standard commercial risks are not covered, the amendment proposed will ensure that the responsibility will not be the tenant's but will lie with the landlord. Particular consideration now needs to be given to whether terrorism should be specified as an insured risk in its own right. Historical definitions of terrorism, making reference to any act of any person acting on behalf of or in connection with any organisation with activities directed towards the overthrowing or influencing of any government *de jure* or *de facto* by force or violence, have now moved on. The Terrorism Act 2000 contains a new definition, which is much wider than the Association of British Insurers Standard Exclusion used by *Pool Re*. From the beginning of 1993, the Association of British Insurers, in consequence of huge payouts following acts of terrorism on mainland Britain, said they would no longer provide cover against acts of terrorism. Clearly, the potential consequences for landlords and tenants were potentially devastating which meant that the government had to intervene with the Reinsurance Act of Terrorism Act 1993.

Essentially, the government accepted an obligation to act as an insurer of last resort for acts of terrorism in place of commercial reinsurers who had decided that the marketplace was no longer for them! Any insurers who now offer cover for acts of terrorism become members of a mutual reinsurance company (*Pool Re Insurance Company* which is known as *Pool Re*) which reinsures all terrorism risks in mainland Britain, cover for which is offered by its insurer members. Additional premiums have to be paid by the insured, and the government in turn, reinsures the insurance company. How long the government is prepared to prop up the system like that is likely to be a political decision as much as anything. On 23 July 2002 the Treasury issued a new statement indicating how Pool Re would react to the catastrophic events and tragedy of 11 September 2001. Various political and industry lobbyists had expressed concern to the Treasury, asking them to make up the gap between the total exclusion being applied to the market generally,

1.22   *'Interest'*   Unless the context requires otherwise, references to 'interest' are references to interest during the period from the date on which the payment is due to the date of payment, both before and after any judgment, at the Interest Rate then prevailing (where the interest rate is defined by reference to a bank base rate) or, should the base rate referred to in **clause 1.23** 'THE INTEREST RATE' cease to exist, at another <u>reasonably comparable </u>rate of interest ~~upon which the Landlord decides~~ <u>closely comparable with the Interest Rate to be agreed between the parties or in default of agreement to be determined by the </u>~~Landlord's~~<u> Accountant acting as an expert and not as an arbitrator</u>

1.23   *'Interest Rate'*   ~~the rate of 2% per year above~~ the base lending rate of [ ] Bank plc or such other <u>major clearing </u>bank as the Landlord <u>(acting reasonably) </u>from time to time nominates in writing

1.24   *'Landlord'*   includes the person or persons from time to time entitled to possession of the Premises when this Lease comes to an end

and the limited cover provided by Pool Re. The changes took effect from 20 August 2002, but at the time of writing there is still no policy wording to consider. However, it is important to be aware of the existence of the proposed changes, many of which came into effect on 1 January 2003. From a tenant"s point of view, it needs to ensure, absolutely, either that terrorism is an insured risk or, in the alternative, to ensure that it has no obligation for damage caused by terrorism. I have inserted a definition of *Terrorism* in the text (see **clause 1.47**). As the tenant is in fact paying for the insurance then, provided his requested amendments are sustainable and reasonable, there is no good reason for the landlord to refuse them.

An alternative would be to insert a definition of 'Uninsured Risks' (see **clause 1.49**) to cover items such as terrorism, flooding (in certain parts of the country now insurers will not offer cover because of recent events and claims histories), heave, landslip and subsidence and to couple this with a provision exempting the tenant from any liability to repair where the damage sustained is caused by an 'Uninsured Risk' as well as an Insured Risk.

1.22   If the interest rate stated in **clause 1.23** ceases to exist for any reason (and who knows how many more banks are going to amalgamate?) then any alternative *interest rate* quoted by the landlord should be something reasonably comparable and not a punitive interest rate linked to some foreign or offshore institution. The proposed amendment caters for this.

1.23   A distinction needs to be drawn between paying interest where the tenant is in default (see definition of 'Default Interest Rate' and **clause 3.17**) and all other cases, for example, the back payment of rent where a rent review is delayed (see paragraph 3.3 of Schedule 4).

1.25	*'Landlord's Expenses'*	the reasonable ~~and proper~~ costs and expenditure (including all charges, commissions, premiums, fees and interest) <u>reasonably and properly</u> paid or incurred, or deemed in accordance with the provisions of Schedule 6 paragraph 2.3 LANDLORD'S EXPENSES. to be paid or incurred, by the Landlord in respect of or incidental to all or any of the Services or otherwise required to be taken into account for the purpose of calculating the Service Charge <u>except those recovered from any insurance policy effected by the Landlord pursuant to</u> **clause 5.2** <u>COVENANT TO INSURE</u>

1.26   *'Liability Period'*

(i)   in the case of [*name of guarantor for Original Tenant*] the period during which the Original Tenant is bound by the tenant covenants of this Lease ~~together with any additional period during which the Original Tenant is liable under an authorised guarantee agreement~~

(ii)   in the case of any guarantor required pursuant to **clause 3.9.5.2** CONDITIONS, the period during which the relevant assignee is bound by the tenant covenants of this Lease ~~together with any additional period during which that assignee is liable under an authorised guarantee agreement~~

(iii)   in the case of any guarantor under an authorised guarantee agreement, the period during which the relevant assignee is bound by the tenant covenants of this Lease and

(iv)   in the case of any guarantor required pursuant to **clause 3.9.8.7** TERMS OF A PERMITTED SUBLEASE, the period during which the relevant assignee of the sublease is bound by the tenant covenants of that sublease.

1.25   This is, arguably, one of the most important amendments that the tenant can make. For some time, based on the decision in *Finchbourne Ltd v Rodrigues* [1976] 3 All ER 581, CA, there was a view that a term would be implied into a lease that service charge expenditure could only be recovered by a landlord to the extent that it was reasonable. In two more recent cases, however, dealing with the recovery of insurance premiums, the courts have refused to imply such a limitation. The cases are *Bandar Property Holdings Ltd v JS Darwen (Successors) Ltd* [1968] 2 All ER 305, *Havenridge Ltd v Boston Dyers Ltd* [1994] 2 EGLR 73, CA and *Berrycroft Management 6 Ltd v Sinclair Gardens Investments (Kensington) Ltd* [1997] 22 EG 14. The only qualification that the courts imposed in both cases was that the expenditure must be properly incurred and not be exorbitant. As the landlords in these cases had settled their premium in the ordinary course of their business, at arm's length and with a reputable insurer, it could not be called into question. The landlord is under no obligation to approach more than one insurer. Inclusion of these words will ensure that your tenant client does not become a test case in determining to resolve whether any such implied term exists in the situation where your client's landlord seeks to be unreasonable in the expenses he claims through the service charge! For the significance of the deletions, refer to Schedule 6 paragraph 2.3. The additions at the end of the clause are self explanatory.

1.26(i) There is currently a healthy debate as to whether or not the guarantor of an original tenant to the lease or the guarantor of any subsequent assignee of the lease can be required, pursuant to the Landlord and Tenant (Covenants) Act 1995, to stand as guarantor to that party when that party himself is, effectively, required to act as a guarantor pursuant to an Authorised Guarantee Agreement. Until the courts are called upon to make a ruling on this point, the guarantor's advisers are best placed to deal with this specifically in the documentation by excluding liability during any such period. The author's view is that any attempt by landlords to require sureties to guarantee an authorised guarantee agreement is likely to fall foul of the anti-avoidance provision contained in section 25 of the Landlord and Tenant (Covenants) Act 1995 but the debate rumbles on. There are certainly many well-respected practitioners who argue that such a requirement can be imposed and so from the tenant or guarantor's point of view it is better not to leave it to chance but to deal with it specifically. A secondary point also arises as to whether a practitioner should be acting for a guarantor as well as the tenant. The safest course of action is to advise the guarantor to take separate legal advice and to record this in writing as the guarantor may choose to ignore your advice. See also the note under the heading 'Parties' on the first page of the commentary.

1.26(ii) The same points apply here as those referred to above in relation to **clause 1.26(i)**.

1.27	*'Losses'*	References to 'losses' are references to <u>all reasonably foreseeable</u> liabilities, damages or losses, awards of damages or compensation, penalties, costs, disbursements or expenses arising from any claim, demand, action or proceedings
1.28	*'1954 Act'*	the Landlord and Tenant Act 1954 and all statutes, regulations and orders included by virtue of **clause 1.46.7** REFERENCES TO STATUTES
1.29	*'1995 Act'*	the Landlord and Tenant (Covenants) Act 1995 and all statutes, regulations and orders included by virtue of **clause 1.46.7** REFERENCES TO STATUTES
1.30	*'Office Covenants'*	the covenants set out in Schedule 5 THE OFFICE COVENANTS
1.31	*'Other buildings'*	References to 'other buildings' are references to all the buildings now or at any time during the Term erected on any adjoining property of the Landlord
1.32	*'Parking Bays'*	those areas of the Building allocated as parking bays
~~**1.33**~~	~~*'Permitted Hours'*~~	~~the period from 9.00 am to 6.00 pm Monday to Friday~~
1.33	<u>*'Permitted Part'*</u>	<u>[the entirety of]/[that part of] the [ ] floor of the Premises</u>
1.34	*'Plan'*	the plan <u>or plans</u> annexed to this Lease <u>and numbered as appropriate</u>
1.35	*'Planning Acts'*	the Town and Country Planning Act 1990 and all statutes, regulations and orders included by virtue of **clause 1.51.7** REFERENCES TO STATUTES
1.36	*'Premises'*	[the first and second floors and part of the third floor of the Building] shown for the purposes of identification only edged red on Plan<u>s 2, 3 and 4</u> and the Included Parking Bays and as more particularly defined in schedule 1 THE PREMISES

1.27 It is important that the tenant tries to limit any losses for which the landlord will seek to make him responsible to those recognised by the general law. The test laid down in *Hadley v Baxendale* (1854) 9 Exch 341 sets down the principle relating to remoteness of damage and the amendment seeks to reflect this.

1.33 The deletion of *Permitted Hours* from the original drafting simply
(deleted) seeks to give the tenant maximum flexibility. Whether this is possible clearly depends on the landlord's management of the building but it is certainly a question the tenant's adviser should be asking.

1.33 While this proposed amendment will not always be relevant, in the
(new) context of this particular specimen lease (where the premises comprise two entire floors and part of another floor of an office building), it may be perfectly logical, and commercial good sense, that the tenant would want to sublet a clearly defined part, ie the whole of any floor or the entire floor area that it has on a particular floor where the floor area does not comprise the entire floor. This will be dealt with in more detail later under the alienation provisions (see **clauses 3.9.7** and **3.9.8**).

1.34 Accurate plans help to avoid dispute. Professionally drawn up and identified plans lessen this likelihood even further. The landlord should be requested to prepare accurate plans, ideally identified by a reference number.

For the Land Registry requirements under the Land Registration Act 2002 (in respect of plans) refer to paragraph 6.7 of Land Registry Practice Guide 40 available on www.landregistry.gov.uk.

In essence, the key points to remember are:

(i) Use metric (not imperial measurements) to two decimal places

(ii) Use a scale of 1:1250 or 1:5000 and state on the plan the scale being used

(iii) Any reduced plans must make it absolutely clear that they are reduced

(iv) Use a north point for orientation

(v) Use a plan that has sufficient details so it can be transferred to an ordnance survey plan

(vi) Mark the extent of the demise clearly and precisely. Do not use a thick line as this can obscure important detail

1.37   *'Rent'*   Until the First Review Date 'the Rent' means the Initial Rent. Thereafter 'the Rent' means the sum ascertained in accordance with schedule 4 THE RENT AND RENT REVIEW. 'The Rent' does not include the Insurance Rent [and the Service Charge], but the term 'the Lease Rents' means both the Rent and the Insurance Rent [and the Service Charge]

1.38   *'Rent Commencement Date'*   [   ]

1.39   *'Retained Parts'*   the parts of the Building that are not let or constructed or adapted for letting, including, without prejudice to the generality of the foregoing, such parts of the main structure, walls, foundations and roofs of the Building as are not included in the Premises and would not be included in premises demised by leases of other units in the Building if let on the same terms as this Lease, and also including office accommodation for the estate manager and any ancillary staff

1.40   *'Review Dates'*   'The First Review Date' means [ ] 'The Review Dates' means the First Review Date [the [ ] day of [ ] in the years 20[ ] and every [5th] anniversary of that date during the Contractual Term] and any other date from time to time specified under Schedule 4, para 3.4 EFFECT OF COUNTER-INFLATION PROVISIONS. References to 'a review date' are reference to any one of the Review Dates

1.41   *'Service Charge'*   the Service Charge Percentage of the Landlord's Expenses

(vii) All parties must execute the plan(s) appropriately

(viii) Plans must not be marked for identification purposes only or bear any other similar legend

(ix) Never seek to include any disclaimer under the Property Misdescriptions Act 1991

(x) Do not use photocopies of plans. Use originals.

1.37   The question of whether 'the Lease Rents' should include 'the Service Charge' is dealt with when considering the suspension of rent under **clause 5.5.2.**

1.38   This will often be left blank in the initial draft submitted by the landlord. The heads of terms must be checked to see if any rent-free period has been negotiated and if they make no reference to a rent-free period then it is, in the author's view, incumbent on the tenant's adviser to check with his client as to whether or not the issue has been raised *especially* if the tenant has or is likely to incur fit out costs in making the premises fit for his intended use.

1.39   As drafted this clause is probably acceptable from the tenant's point of view. It ensures that tenants or occupiers of let units do not end up paying the service charge for unlet units thereby, effectively, subsidising such units. If the definition does not make this absolutely clear, it would need amendment to reflect this. The critical words are '...*not let or constructed or adapted for letting...*' which are relevant in respect of the Service Charge provisions in Schedule 6. Paragraph 1.3 of Schedule 6 puts the matter beyond dispute for the tenant's benefit so that it is important to ensure that his point is covered in the drafting.

1.40   As originally drafted, there is an argument that as a matter of construction this clause by virtue of the definition of '*the Term*' (which includes any holding-over or statutory continuation tenancy (see **clause 1.43**)) enables the landlord to implement what is in effect a 'penultimate day' rent review, although in reality this date may be the first day of any holding-over period where the tenant remains in occupation pursuant to the Landlord and Tenant Act 1954. The amendment ensures that this will not happen. Landlords recognise that there may be a considerable gap between the expiry of the contractual term granted by the lease and the date on which the statutory tenancy ultimately comes to an end. Landlords will argue that by holding over under a statutory tenancy, the tenant may benefit from a historic low rent for as long as possible. The tenant should argue, however, against a penultimate day rent review on the ground that statute provides adequate protection for the landlord by virtue of the interim rent mechanism introduced by section 24A of the Landlord and Tenant Act 1954 as amended by the Regulatory Reform (Business Tenancies) (England & Wales) Order 2003. This enables the landlord to make an application to the court for an

1.42   *'Service Charge Percentage'*   [   ]% subject to the provisions for variation contained in Schedule 6 clause 2.6 VARIATION OF THE SERVICE CHARGE PERCENTAGE

1.43   *'Services'*   the services, facilities and amenities specified in Schedule 6 paragraph 3 THE SERVICES

1.44   *'Surveyor'*   [   ] or any person who is or firm the majority of whose partners are, Fellows or Associates of the Royal Institution of Chartered Surveyors [or Associates or Fellows of the Incorporated Society of Valuers and Auctioneers] appointed by the Landlord in his place. The Surveyor may be an employee of the Landlord or a Group Company. The expression 'the Surveyor' includes the person or firm appointed by the Landlord to collect the Lease Rents

1.45   *'Tenant'*   includes any person who is for the time being bound by the tenant covenants of this Lease

1.46   *'Term'*   the Contractual Term [and any period of holding-over or extension or continuance of the Contractual Term by statute or common law]

1.[47]   *'Terrorism'*   the use or threat (for the purpose of advancing a political, religious or ideological course) of action which (a) involves serious violence against a person, (b) involves serious damage to property, (c) endangers the life of a person, or (d) creates a serious risk to the health or safety of the public or a section of the public

interim rent to be paid. The practical procedural steps that apply to an interim rent application and the basis on which an interim rent is fixed are outside the scope of this book but the mechanism is there to ensure that the landlord gets a proper return during this period of holding over by the tenant. The tenant's adviser should therefore strenuously resist any attempts by the landlord to implement a penultimate day rent review. Under the proposed reforms to the Landlord and Tenant Act 1954 as amended by the Regulatory Reform (Business Tenancies) (England & Wales) Order 2003, the tenant, as well as the landlord, will be able to apply for an interim rent. In addition, other significant changes are to be made relating both to when the interim rent becomes payable and the calculation of this rent.

1.42   The same comments apply here as those suggested in relation to **clause 1.20**.

1.44   The same principles referred to in **clause 1.1** apply here. Depending on the nature and complexity of the building of which the premises form part and the likely management involvement associated with it, it is suggested that the stated professional criteria will give the tenant the additional comfort that any surveying duties should be carried out properly.

1.46   The square brackets have been incorporated here as a reminder that if the lease is *contracted out* from the security of tenure provisions granted by Part II of the Landlord and Tenant Act 1954 the words between them need to be deleted. It is also vitally important to consider the impact of the words in brackets on an original tenant (or assignee) under a pre-1 January 1996 Lease when the original tenant or assignee is no longer the tenant at the expiry of the contractual term. If the present tenant 'holds over' the original tenant's liability expires at the end of the contractual term (as does that of any assignee no longer the present tenant) *only* if the wording in brackets is *not* included or this liability is specifically excluded elsewhere (*City of London Corpn v Fell* [1994] 1 AC 458, HL).

1.47   This definition is taken from the Terrorism Act 2000, and is the best definition the author has come across.

1.48   *'this Lease'*   unless expressly stated to the contrary, the expression 'this Lease' includes any document stated to be supplemental to or collateral with this document or entered into in accordance with this document

1.[49]   *'Uninsured Risks'*   a risk or an Insured Risk against which insurance cover is not generally available or ceases to be available for properties such as the Premises or is available only on terms or subject to conditions making it unreasonable in all the circumstances to effect insurance against that risk

1.50   *'VAT'*   value added tax or any other tax of a similar nature and, unless otherwise expressly stated, all references to rents or other sums payable by the Tenant are exclusive of VAT

1.51.1   Words importing one gender include all other genders; words importing the singular include the plural and vice versa and any reference to persons includes not only individuals but companies or other corporate bodies

1.51.2   The clause, paragraph and schedule headings and the table of contents do not form part of this document and are not to be taken into account in its construction or interpretation

1.51.3   Any reference in this document to a clause, subclause, paragraph, subparagraph or schedule without further designation is to be construed as a reference to the clause, subclause, paragraph or schedule to this document so numbered

1.51.4   References to any right of the Landlord to have access to the Premises are to be construed as extending to any head landlord or mortgagee of the Premises (where the headlease or mortgage grants such rights of access to the head landlord or mortgagee) and to all persons authorised in writing by the Landlord (or any head landlord or mortgagee having rights of access) including agents, professional advisers, contractors, workmen and others

1.48   This amendment is self-explanatory. The tenant would not want to be subject to obligations, liabilities or other onerous provisions brought in by a document (for example a licence or side letter) which was not clearly expressed to be supplemental to the lease itself.

1.49   See the footnote of **clause 1.21**. The British Property Federation (the BPF) has received reports that tenants negotiating new leases will not accept 'the Uninsured Risks' on the basis that they have no capital interest in the buildings. BPF members are reporting losing potential lettings as a result and also that the additional risk is being cited in rent review negotiations as a reason for payment of a lower rent. The BPF Model Clauses do not, however, address this issue as their consultation 'has shown that there is no industry wide consensus on the issue'.

1.50   The words deleted are very vague and potentially expose a tenant to an additional unknown and unquantified liability. The landlord may well require reinstatement of this clause and this may be acceptable to a tenant provided such a tax simply replaced VAT and did not impose any additional liability.

   Recommendation 5 of the Code: Rent and value added tax: *Where alternative lease terms are offered, different rents should be appropriately priced for each set of terms. The landlord should disclose the VAT status of the property and the tenant should take professional advice as to whether any VAT charged on rent and other charges is recoverable.*

1.51.1 This amendment is self-explanatory.

1.51.2 This addition is self-explanatory, ensuring there is no question mark over derivative parties' exercise of any rights granted in this lease to the tenant.

1.51.4 This amendment is self-explanatory. These additional words should be included so that the clause applies only where the consent of a mortgagee or head landlord is required under the terms of a mortgage or head lease that has been created before the lease is entered into. In addition to this, the prudent tenant should request a copy of the relevant document to ascertain if the rights of the mortgagee or head landlord do, in fact, exist. Unless these words are included the landlord could, by subsequently creating a mortgage or a head lease, bring about a situation where consent could be refused in circumstances in which it would otherwise have been unreasonable so to do. The need for mortgagee's or head landlord's consent is particularly relevant in the context of alienation where the effect on the tenant's ability to assign or sublet could be adverse to the tenant's interest at the date of the lease.

1.51.5   <u>References to any rights exercisable by the Tenant shall be construed as being exercisable by the Tenant, any sub-tenant or sub-tenants and all persons properly authorised by them</u>

1.51.6   References to 'the last year of the Term' are references to the actual last year of the Term howsoever it determines, and references to the 'end of the Term' are references to the end of the Term whensoever and howsoever it determines

1.51.7   Unless expressly stated to the contrary any references to a specific statute include <u>(save where in consequence of the same any additional or more onerous liability may be imposed on the Tenant or Guarantor)</u> any statutory extension or modification, amendment or re-enactment of that statute and any regulations or orders made under that statute, and any general reference to a statute includes any regulations or orders made under that statute

1.52   *Terms from the 1995 Act*

Where the expressions 'landlord covenants', 'tenant covenants', or 'authorised guarantee agreement' are used in this Lease they are to have the meaning given by the 1995 Act section 28(1).

1.53   *Interpretation of consent and approved*

1.53.1   Prior written consent or approval

References to 'consent of the Landlord' or words to similar effect are references to a prior written consent signed by ~~or on behalf of~~ the Landlord and references to the need for anything to be 'approved by the Landlord' or words to similar effect are references to the need for a prior written approval by ~~or on behalf of~~ the Landlord

1.53.2   Consent or approval of mortgagee or head landlord

Any provisions in this Lease referring to the consent or approval of the Landlord are to be construed as also requiring the consent or approval of any mortgagee of the Premises and any head landlord, where that consent is required <u>under the terms of a mortgage or headlease in existence at the date of this Lease</u>. Nothing in this Lease is to be construed as imposing any obligation on a mortgagee or head landlord not to refuse any consent or approval unreasonably

1.53.3   References to 'the last year of the Term' are references to the actual last year of the Term howsoever it determines, and references to the 'end of the Term' are references to the end of the Term whensoever and howsoever it determines

1.51.7 The proposed amendment here seeks to draw a line in the sand so that the tenant's liability is established at the commencement of the lease for the duration of the term and is not subsequently increased following statutory or other legislative changes during the lifetime of the lease. This is unlikely to prove acceptable to the landlord but nonetheless the tenant may consider it appropriate to raise the issue.

1.53.1 The last thing that a tenant needs is a dispute as to whether or not a person or party signing any form of consent or approval has the relevant authority to do so. The amendment seeks to avoid this.

Recommendation 12 of the Code: Request for consents: When seeking a consent from the landlord, the tenant should supply full information about his/her proposal. The landlord should respond without undue delay and should where practicable give the tenant an estimate of the costs that the tenant will have to pay. The landlord should ensure that the request is passed promptly to any superior landlord or mortgagee whose agreement is needed and should give details to the tenant so that any problems can be speedily resolved.

1.53.2 The same arguments apply here as those referred to in **clause 1.51.4** above.

1.54   *Joint and several liability*

Where any party to this Lease for the time being comprises two or more persons, obligations expressed or implied to be made by or with that party are deemed to be made by or with the persons comprising that party jointly and severally

1.55   *Obligation not to permit or suffer*

Any covenant by the Tenant not to do anything includes an obligation not to knowingly permit or knowingly suffer that thing to be done by another person |

1.56   *Interpretation of 'the Premises'*

In the absence of any provision to the contrary, references to 'the Premises' include any part of the Premises

2   **DEMISE**

2.1   The Landlord demises the Premises to the Tenant [with [full] | [limited] title guaranteed] together with the rights specified in | Schedule 2 THE RIGHTS GRANTED but excepting and reserving to the Landlord the rights specified in Schedule 3 THE RIGHTS RESERVED, to hold to the Tenant for the Contractual Term subject to~~all rights, easements, privileges, restrictions, covenants and stipulations of whatever nature affecting the Premises including any~~ those matters contained or referred to | in Schedule 7 THE SUBJECTIONS yielding and paying to the Landlord:

2.1.1   the Rent,~~without any deduction or set off,~~ by equal quarterly | payments in advance on the usual quarter days in every year and proportionately for any period of less than a year, the first such payment, being a proportionate sum in respect of the period from and including the Rent Commencement Date to and including the day before the quarter day next after the Rent Commencement Date, [to be paid on the date of this document] and

1.54   Sometimes this clause will not, intentionally on the part of the land-lord, make reference to the landlord. It should be amended to ensure it refers to *all* parties to the lease.

1.55   This additional word *'knowingly'* is wonderfully effective for the tenant. Landlords may be hard pushed to argue that a tenant should be responsible for something he knows nothing about and may accept that the tenant should not be under strict liability. While the relative bargaining strengths will be all important (as ever) the tenant should press strongly for such an amendment.

2   DEMISE

2.1   The tenant would be ill-advised to enter into a lease without know-ing what encumbrances affect the premises at the time he takes the lease. These should be clearly set out in a schedule. The general wording which has been deleted is far too wide ranging and, in the author's view, absolutely unacceptable. As the landlord is not obliged to deduce title (but he can, of course, always be asked to do so and in some cases the tenant should insist) there may be provi-sions contained in the freehold title or a head lease which render the tenant's proposals for the premises not only unviable but illegal. If the landlord insists on such a provision as originally drafted, the tenant should insist that title is deduced. There is a strong arguable case that if the tenant has agreed to pay the landlord's legal costs in connection with the grant of the lease (see clause 3.27) then at the very least this additional work should be paid for by the landlord. Under the provisions of the Land Registration Act 2002 (s 44) leas-es for seven years or more will become compulsorily registrable and in the case of any such lease the landlord will be obliged to deduce title.

2.1.1   Deduction and set-off are valuable weapons in the tenant's armoury (see *Lee Parker v Izzet* [1971] 3 All ER 1099 and *Muscat v Smith* [2003] EWCA Civ 962) and, while many landlords (particularly institutional landlords) insist on what have become known as *clear leases* (ie leases where they are guaranteed that every month or quar-ter they will receive their rent clear of any deductions), the author considers that there is no good reason why the rights of deduction or set-off should be lost if the landlord has assumed important obliga-tions such as repair and is in breach of his contractual leasehold obli-gations. The tenant can argue that every provision in the lease which involves expenditure by the landlord is mirrored by a provision

2.1.2   by way of further rent the Service Charge payable in accordance with Schedule 6 THE SERVICE CHARGE and the
Insurance Rent payable ~~on~~ within [21] days of demand in |
accordance with clause 5.4 PAYMENT OF THE INSURANCE
RENT

3   THE TENANT'S COVENANTS

The Tenant covenants with the Landlord to observe and perform the requirements of this clause 3

3.1   *Rent*

3.1.1   *Payment of the Lease Rents*

The Tenant must pay the Lease Rents on the days and in the
manner set out in this Lease~~, and must not exercise or seek to~~ |
~~exercise any right or claim to withhold rent, or any right or~~
~~claim to legal or equitable set off~~ (except where made pur- |
suant to any statute)

3.1.2   *Payment by banker's order*

If so reasonably required in writing by the Landlord, the Tenant |
must pay the Lease Rents by banker's order or credit transfer
to any bank and account in the UK that the Landlord reason- |
ably nominates from time to time

requiring the tenant to reimburse the landlord for such expenditure and this argument should be used to reinstate the right to deduction and set-off except, perhaps, where as is sometimes the case, the only obligation on the landlord is for quiet enjoyment! In any event there could be instances where the tenant must make deductions (eg if the landlord is based offshore and tax becomes payable directly to the Inland Revenue). As an absolute minimum, therefore, the words '...*(save where required by statute)*...' should be included.

2.1.2   Periods of grace are not unusual and are generally commercially acceptable to landlords so that interest provisions do not immediately become operative. If this is common practice there is no reason why it should not be enshrined and become a contractual provision.

3   THE TENANT'S COVENANTS

3.1.1   Although the words '...*yielding and paying*...' referred to in **clause 2.1** actually imply a covenant on the part of the tenant to pay the rent, a specific covenant is invariably included. As has been stated in relation to **clause 2.1.1** the ability to *set off* is a valuable weapon in the tenant's limited armoury. Landlords, particularly institutional landlords, are always keen to have a *clear* lease, meaning that all rental due is received gross. However, there can be little compelling argument from the landlord's point of view as to why, if a tenant has to spend his own money complying with what is contractually a landlord's obligation, it should not have the right to set off (meaning it can deduct from the rent and other sums due to the landlord the cost of so complying). Landlords will no doubt argue that tenants have suitable remedies for breach of contract if the landlord is in breach but this involves the expense and delay of making a claim and potential litigation on the part of the tenant. The self-help remedy of *set-off* is much more appealing from a tenant's point of view and should be argued for strongly, especially where this may be permitted by statute. An example of this would be paying the rent net of basic rate income tax to a non-UK resident landlord (unless paid to a UK-based agent when the rent would still need to be paid gross). Landlords should be pressed for compelling reasons as to why this right should not be available. A clause that provides that the rent is payable '*without any deductions*' will not exclude the right of set-off. See *Connaught Restaurants Limited v Indoor Leisure Limited* [1994] 1 WLR 501.

3.1.2   If rental payments are made by banker's order (by agreement) then it is important that the tenant does what it can to ensure that his accounts department is not inadvertently notified to send money to an offshore account. If a request for offshore payments is received then such payments must be made net of basic rate tax. If rental payments are made gross (in error) then it is difficult, if not impossible, for the tenant to recover this tax element of the rent. The tenant would still, however, have to account to the Inland Revenue for

3.2   *Outgoings and VAT*

3.2.1   Outgoings exclusive to the Premises

The Tenant must pay, and must indemnify the Landlord against:

3.2.1.1   all rates, taxes, assessments, duties, charges, impositions and outgoings (save those of a capital nature) that are now or may at any time during the Term be charged, assessed or imposed on the Premises or on the ~~owner or~~ occupier of them (excluding any payable by the Landlord occasioned by receipt of the Lease Rents or by any disposition of or dealing with this Lease or ownership of any interest reversionary to the interest created by it)~~provided that if, after the end of the Term, the Landlord suffers loss of any rating relief applicable to empty premises because the relief has been allowed to the Tenant in respect of a period before the end of the Term, then the Tenant must make good such loss to the Landlord~~

3.2.1.2   all VAT from time to time charged on the Lease Rents or other sums payable by the Tenant under this Lease provided that the Landlord shall have previously delivered to the Tenant a valid VAT invoice addressed to the Tenant for the full amount

3.2.1.3   all VAT incurred in relation to any costs that the Tenant is obliged to pay or in respect of which he is required to indemnify the Landlord under the terms of this Lease provided that the Landlord shall have previously delivered to the Tenant a valid VAT invoice addressed to the Tenant for the full amount

the basic rate tax payments which means a double payment. The amendments to the clause seek to ensure this will not happen. One argument for deletion of this clause in its entirety is to make the landlord aware that acceptance of such a payment by a landlord could in certain circumstances amount to a waiver of tenant's breach of covenant. The author has often used this argument successfully as landlords view deletion of the clause as the lesser of two 'evils'.

3.2.1.1 A number of issues arise in relation to this clause. Firstly, on a shorter-term lease, the tenant should seek to ensure that any capital outgoings relating to the premises fall to be paid by the landlord. The tenant should not be seen to be funding *betterment* and giving the landlord back something more valuable than that which he granted. It is not easy to identify when a shorter-term lease becomes a longer-term lease such that a tenant could be reasonably expected to be responsible for outgoings of a capital nature, but the author would suggest that anything over a five- or six-year term may well fall into this latter category. Secondly, it is essential that a tenant ensures that any corporation tax or income tax payable by the landlord as a result of the receipt of the rent or any other payments due under the lease similarly fall to be paid by the landlord. Thirdly, any taxes falling due on the landlord's dealings with any interest in reversion to the lease again should be payable by the landlord. As a final point, the tenant should delete reference to the loss of rating relief. If the landlord gives up control of the property to the tenant for the term created by the lease then if, in the commercial interests of the tenant, the tenant decides to vacate the premises and obtains rating relief, there is no reason why he should be penalised for this by having to reimburse the landlord on expiry of the lease.

Recommendation 19 of the Code: Business Rates: *Tenants or other ratepayers should consider if their business rates assessment is correct or whether they need to make an appeal. They should refer to the DTLR Business Rates – a Guide or obtain advice from a rating specialist. RICS provides a free rating helpline service and advice is available also from the Institute of Revenues Rating and Valuation (IRRV).*

3.2.1.2 Current VAT legislation states that the provider of a service must provide a valid VAT invoice in relation to any input tax incurred by the paying party. All too often difficulties are encountered with VAT invoices not being available at the time payments are made and often they never materialise. This is particularly relevant when premiums are paid on assignments of leases. The tenant's (or assignee's) solicitor must ensure that such an invoice is available before or at the time payment is made. The only bargaining stick which the tenant has is to be able to say that he is not going to meet the payment until the invoice is available. Once the payment has been made there is no incentive for the landlord to provide the invoice.

3.2.2 Outgoings assessed on the Premises and other property

The Tenant must pay, and must indemnify the Landlord against, the proportion reasonably and properly attributable to the Premises (to be determined from time to time by the Surveyor, acting as an expert and not as an arbitrator) of all rates, taxes, assessments, duties, charges, impositions and outgoings save those of a capital nature that are now or at any time during the Term may be charged, assessed or imposed on the Premises and any other property, including the rest of the Building any adjoining property of the Landlord, or on the owner or occupier of them and it

3.3 *Cost of services consumed*

The Tenant must pay to the suppliers, and indemnify the Landlord against, all charges for electricity, water, gas, telecommunications and other services consumed or used by the Tenant at or in relation to the Premises, including meter rents and standing charges, and must comply with the lawful requirements and regulations of the respective suppliers of which the Tenant has received written notice

3.4 *Repair, cleaning and decoration*

3.4.1 Repair of the Premises

The Tenant must repair the Premises and keep them in ~~good condition~~ repair, damages by an Insured Risk, or [Terrorism (whether an Insured Risk or not)] [or an Uninsured Risk excepted] save to the extent that the insurance money is irrecoverable due to any act or default of the Tenant or anyone at the Premises expressly or by implication with his authority and under his control PROVIDED ALWAYS the Tenant shall not be obliged by this or any other obligation contained anywhere in this Lease to put the Premises into any better state of repair and condition than that evidenced by the Schedule of Condition attached hereto and initialled by or on behalf of the parties to this Lease and PROVIDED FURTHER that nothing in this Lease shall be construed as obliging the Tenant to remedy any Inherent Defect of whose existence the Tenant has during the Term, notified the Landlord or any want of repair which is attributable to such Inherent Defect, which manifests itself at any time during the Term

3.2.1.3   Exactly the same comments apply here as in **clause 3.2.1.2** above.

3.2.2   The same point can be made here concerning outgoings of a capital nature as has been made in relation to **clause 3.2.1.1** above. The tenant has the protection, if the tenant's adviser has made the appropriate amendments to the draft lease (see **clause 1.41**), of knowing that the surveyor will act in an ethical and proper manner. The addition of the word *reasonably* further enforces this obligation.

3.3   It is unlikely that anyone other than the tenant will have used the services but just in case there is a question mark over consumption, for example, of water, this amendment at least gives the tenant a chance to argue with the landlord. The second amendment is self-explanatory. The tenant cannot be expected to comply with issues of which he is not aware. While as occupier he is very likely to have been notified by the suppliers, sometimes, inadvertently, freeholders can be contacted directly by statutory undertakers and other service providers, and the second amendment is designed to ensure that any such information received by the landlord is passed onto the tenant.

3.4.1   This clause has been drafted originally as a standard tenant's full repairing obligation. There may be compelling reasons why, in the circumstances of the letting in question, this is not appropriate, eg a short-term letting or a letting of a dilapidated building. In the context of the lease we are considering (a lease of a suite of offices comprising only a part of a building), this repairing obligation relates only to the interior of the premises. If it is not appropriate for whatever reason to have a tenant's full repairing obligation (because, for example, the windows are in need of replacement or the central heating is archaic), the amendment suggested is an obvious way to mitigate the harshness of such a clause on the tenant. The only downside to this amendment is that it does involve the preparation of a schedule of condition at additional cost. As the tenant is the one likely to be requesting such a schedule the landlord may well turn the argument around and say that if the tenant wants a schedule of condition he must pay for it. However, in the context of potential dilapidation claims during or at the end of the term, a few hundred pounds paid to a surveyor to prepare such a schedule may well be money well spent and a very useful insurance policy. The schedule will usually comprise a portfolio of photographs with a written commentary or, in other instances, may be undertaken on a video camera with a narrative. It is essential that whichever method is adopted a final product is agreed with the landlord. There should be little room for dispute as it should merely be a record of factual matters. The tenant's adviser should delete the word 'condition' in the light of the

decision in *Welsh v Greenwich London Borough Council* [2000] 49 EG 118, CA when the court held that 'condition' was intended to mark a different concept and make a significant addition to that conveyed by the word 'repair'. The tenant should also delete references in the covenant to repair to words imposing a greater obligation such as 'replace', 'renew', 'rebuild', 'reconstruct', 'reinstate', 'make good defects' and other similar words which will have the effect of widening the obligation to repair. A landlord should appreciate that an onerous repairing obligation can seriously rebound on him at a rent review or lease renewal. In *Norwich Union Life v British Railway Board* [1987] 2 EGLR 137 an obligation to 'rebuild' resulted in the rent on review being discounted by 27.5%. It is a question of fact and degree and a consideration of all the circumstances, in particular the state of the building and the nature of the services, which will dictate whether or not the tenant tries to push matters further and provide that the landlord will be responsible for making good any defects noted in such a schedule (eg the roof) if it became unfit for use and also that the tenant is not responsible, via the service charge, for repairs and/or improvements to the building of which the particular demised premises form part. This is likely to prove less attractive to the landlord but a tenant should, nevertheless, attempt to mitigate the potential harshness of having to contribute large sums via the service charge to, for example, repairing or improving the structure of the building. (See para 2.3.2 of Schedule 6.)

Other matters which will need specific consideration in the context of both the repairing clause and the extent to which a tenant must contribute to repairs via the service charge are terrorism, possibly uninsured risks, contamination generally (see paras [47] to [68] of Division J Ross: Commercial Leases and Precedent 30 in Ross: Commercial Leases) and structural and inherent defects (see para 2.3.2 of Schedule 6). The author would always suggest that disrepair due to terrorism or uninsured risks (whether insured against or not) should be excluded specifically from both the tenant's repairing covenant and, perhaps, depending on the location of the premises, maybe 'flooding' (where no cover is available). An environmental search will reveal whether a property falls within a floodplain; the appearance of a site within an area marked as a floodplain could have a significant effect on its insurance status. The same considerations also apply to the service charge heads of expenditure (see para 2.3.2 of Schedule 6), while disrepair which manifests itself as a result of inherent or structural defect is more a matter of negotiation, as referred to in the proviso to **clause 3.4.1** and the note on this clause in the case of a new build. Collateral warranties may be available to an original tenant of new-built premises which would mitigate the hardship of the repairs in such circumstances, but a tenant would still then need to prove negligence on the part of the professionals involved in the design and construction of the premises. An alternative would be to accept an obligation from the landlord and its successor (by way of a covenant) to pursue the professionals in an action for negligence under their Letters of Appointment or building contract. Ideally the tenant would want

3.4.2   Replacement of landlord's fixtures

The Tenant must replace any landlord's fixtures and fittings in the Premises that are beyond <u>economic</u> repair ~~at any time during or~~ at the end of the Term <u>(fair wear and tear excluded).</u>

3.4.3   Cleaning and tidying

The Tenant must keep the Premises clean and tidy and clear of all rubbish

3.4.4   The Included Parking Bays

3.4.4.1   Care of the Included Parking Bays

The Tenant must ~~keep the Included Parking Bays adequately marked out, surfaced, in good condition and free from weeds, and must~~ use them for car parking only

3.4.4.2   Storage on the Included Parking Bays

The Tenant must not store anything on the Included Parking Bays or bring anything onto them that <u>is likely to cause a legal nuisance</u> ~~is or might become untidy, unclean, unsightly or in any way detrimental to the Building or the area generally~~

3.4.4.3   Rubbish on the Included Parking Bays

The Tenant must not deposit any waste, rubbish or refuse on the Included Parking Bays or place any receptacle for waste, rubbish or refuse on them

3.4.4.4   Caravans on the Included Parking Bays

The Tenant must not keep or store any caravan or movable dwelling on the Included Parking Bays

no liability for disrepair arising from any such manifestation. It is much better to exclude it in its entirety if at all possible.

Recommendation 7 of the Code: Repairs and services: *The tenant's repairing obligations, and any repairs costs included in service charges, should be appropriate to the length of the term and the condition and age of the property at the start of the lease. Where appropriate the landlord should consider appropriately priced alternatives to full repairing terms.*

Recommendation 18 of the Code: Repairs: *Tenants should take the advice of a property professional about their repairing obligations near the end of the term of the lease and also immediately upon receiving a notice to repair or a schedule of dilapidations.*

3.4.2   This amendment is self-explanatory. The tenant should have obtained, through the replies to his preliminary enquiries, a full listing of what the landlord considers to be his fixtures and fittings at the premises so the tenant knows *exactly* what such obligations relate to. There is a point when repairs become economically unviable and the only real alternative is replacement. This amendment attempts to give the tenant as much scope as possible to go down the cheaper route. Items such as lifts or air conditioning units, plant and area carpets can be extremely expensive to replace. The proposed addition seeks to strike a fair balance between the two extremes.

3.4.4.1   The deletion here is intended only when the lease is for a shorter term (see **clause 3.2**). With a shorter-term letting a tenant will not want the expense of having to undertake the works referred to in the clause as originally drawn. Again, much will depend on the individual facts of each particular letting but on a short-term letting these requirements are unduly onerous. It is important to bear in mind that if car parking bays in a somewhat dilapidated state are actually included in the definition of the premises, photographs or video footage of the bays should be included in a schedule of condition to ensure that any repair costs do not fall on the tenant.

3.4.4.2   The proposed amendment is intended to spell out contractually what can and cannot be done. The deleted words are very subjective and will mean different things to different people. The amendment attempts to put on a legal footing those things that the tenant cannot do by reference to the tort of nuisance. While a court would have to decide what is or might be untidy, unclean, unsightly or in any way detrimental to the building or the area generally if the matter was litigated, the author suspects that this is an area fraught with potential conflicting views by the parties and that such widely subjective provisions are best avoided.

3.4.5   Decoration

The Tenant must redecorate the Premises in a good and work-manlike manner, with appropriate materials of good quality, and to the reasonable satisfaction of the Surveyor in each of the Decorating Years and in the last year of the Term, any change in the tints, colours and patterns of the decoration to be approved by the Landlord (such approval not to be unreasonably withheld or delayed) PROVIDED ALWAYS that the Tenant shall not be obliged by this or any other provision in this Lease to decorate the Premises more than once in any three (3) year period nor shall the covenant relating to the last year of the Term apply where the Tenant has redecorated the Premises less than [18] months before the end of the Term

3.5   ~~Waste and~~ Alterations

3.5.1   ~~Waste,~~ additions and alterations

The Tenant must not ~~commit any waste,~~ make any addition to the Premises, unite the Premises with any adjoining premises, or make any structural alteration to the Premises except as permitted by the provisions of this clause 3.5

3.5.2   Preconditions for alterations

The Tenant must not make any structural alterations to the Premises unless he first:

3.5.2.1   obtains and complies with the necessary consents of the competent authorities and pays their charges for them

3.5.2.2   makes an application to the Landlord for consent, supported by reasonable drawings and where appropriate a reasonable specification in duplicate ~~prepared by an architect, or a member of some other appropriate profession, who must supervise the work throughout to completion~~

3.5.2.3   pays the reasonable and proper fees of the Landlord (and where required by any headlease or mortgage), any head landlord, any mortgagee and their respective professional advisers

3.5.2.4   enters into any reasonable covenants the Landlord reasonably requires as to the execution and reinstatement of the alterations and

3.5.2.5   obtains the consent of the Landlord such consent not to be unreasonably withheld or delayed

In the case of any works of a substantial nature, the Landlord may where circumstances might reasonably require it require

3.4.5   The first amendment is designed to ensure that the landlord is not unreasonable in its decorative requirements while the second attempts to ensure, particularly towards the end of the term, that the obligation to decorate is not unduly onerous by requiring it to be done more than once in such a short period of time that the second set of decorations are not, in the circumstances, really required. The author has stated as long a period as possible which is likely to prove acceptable to the landlord, but it may well be that the landlord would attempt to negotiate the period down.

Recommendation 10 of the Code: Alterations and changes of use: *Landlord's control over alterations and changes of use should not be more restrictive than is necessary to protect the value of the premises and any adjoining or neighbouring premises of the landlord. At the end of the lease the tenant should not be required to remove and make good permitted alterations unless this is reasonably required.*

3.5.1   Waste is very widely defined in legal terms and includes voluntary waste, permissive waste, ameliorative waste and equitable waste (topics beyond the scope of this book). In practice demolition and alterations to buildings will often amount to be waste and improvements can amount to 'ameliorative' waste! For this reason it is suggested that a covenant not to commit waste has no relevance in a modern lease and should be deleted. The likelihood of the tenant wanting to make alterations to any particular premises is always going to be a question of fact and degree and therefore accepting an absolute prohibition on alteration is not advisable. If a qualified prohibition is included it is important that the tenant realises that (unless the alteration constitutes 'an improvement' by virtue of s 19(2) of the Landlord and Tenant Act 1927) there is no statutorily implied term which states that such consent cannot unreasonably be withheld. In a letting such as this (office space) there is always going to be the likelihood of the tenant wanting to put up and take down internal demountable stud partitioning walls to make the best use of the available space (see new **clause 3.5.3**). Every time the tenant wishes to do this, he does not want to have to go to the landlord for formal consent with the cost and delays associated with such applications. When the landlord is letting an area of office space (as in this circumstance), there is no detriment to the landlord if the internal partitions are being moved around providing that if *reasonably* required at the end of the term, the tenant is under an obligation to give the landlord back the premises in the state in which he took them. Structural alterations are, however, a completely different matter and it is perfectly reasonable for a landlord to exercise a high degree of control over such structural alterations. The amendment to **clause 3.5.1** attempts to reflect this. One statutory provision which is often overlooked is s 3 of the Landlord and Tenant Act 1927, which can help a tenant to circumvent any attempts by the landlord to impose an absolute prohibition on alterations. It contains a procedure for obtaining consent from the landlord (or if the landlord will not consent, the Court) for improvements. Unlike s 19(2) of the 1927 Act (which only applies

the Tenant to provide, before starting the works, ~~adequate~~ <u>reasonable</u> security in the form of a deposit of money or the provision of a bond as assurance to the Landlord that any works he permits from time to time will be fully completed.

3.5.3   <u>Internal partitions</u>

<u>Without prejudice to the provisions of this clause 3.5, the Tenant may install, alter and remove internal demountable partitions if he gives notice of the works to the Landlord within one month of completion of the works and ensures that there is no disruption of the services in, to and through the Premises</u>

3.5.3   ~~Removal of alterations~~

~~At the end of the Term, if so requested by the Landlord, the Tenant must remove any additions, alterations or improvements made to the Premises, and must make good any loss occasioned by such removal~~

to qualified covenants) s 3 may be used where the lease contains an absolute prohibition against tenants' alterations. It is a useful weapon in the tenant's armoury, and although it involves a slightly convoluted and complex procedure, it is certainly a useful weapon in the negotiating process to argue against an absolute prohibition.

3.5.2.2   The amendments to this clause are designed to minimise the cost to the tenant so far as possible. It may not be necessary, in the context to the proposed works, for the drawings and specification to be prepared by an architect or other professionally qualified person. Inclusion of the word '*reasonable*', twice, gives the landlord the necessary protection. Landlords also need to be conscious of the decision reached by the Court of Appeal in the case of *Prudential Assurance Co Limited v Mount Eden Land Limited* [1997] 1 EGLR 37 where a letter issued by the landlord's agents giving consent in the form of a letter but being expressed to be subject to a formal licence being created, was held by the Court of Appeal actually to constitute a consent to the alterations.

3.5.2.3   The fetter on fees is self-explanatory. The second amendment ensures that the tenant is able, at the time he enters into the lease, to know the extent of the obligations he has in relation to the cost of obtaining consent from any head landlord or mortgagee.

3.5.2.4   The amendments here are intended to ensure that the tenant is not held to ransom by the landlord in relation to the proposed alterations. If the landlord can sustain reasonable arguments with reasonable reasons as to why the alterations should be undertaken in a particular way or why there should be reinstatement, the tenant is likely to have little choice but to accept these; but the tenant should not be at the whim of the landlord in this respect.

3.5.2.5   This amendment which is self-explanatory and is an important one because without it a landlord may frustrate a tenant by not responding at all or by acting in a dilatory fashion. The amendment to the final paragraph of the clause seeks simply to introduce, once again, an element of fairness into the conduct of the landlord.

3.5.3   As explained at **clause 3.5.1**, this new clause seeks to differentiate
(new)   between alterations of a structural and non-structural nature by ensuring that a tenant can install and remove partitioning without requiring the prior consent of the landlord. The final part of the clause should give the landlord all the protection he needs.

3.5.3   Deletion of this clause is designed to ensure that any alterations
(deleted) undertaken and the requirement for reinstatement are considered on their own merits at the time consent for them is sought by the tenant. It is unlikely to prove acceptable to the landlord. The compromise would be to vary the covenant so that the obligation on the part of the tenant to reinstate only applies if this is reasonable. This is a Code recommendation too.

3.5.4   Connection to the Conduits

The Tenant must not make any connection with the Conduits that serve the Premises without the Landlord's consent such consent not to be unreasonably withheld or delayed

3.6   *Aerials signs and advertisements*

3.6.1   Masts and wires

The Tenant must not erect any pole, ~~or~~ mast, satellite dish or other telecommunications receiving equipment or install any cable or wire on the Premises, whether in connection with telecommunications or otherwise without the Landlord's consent such consent not to be unreasonably withheld or delayed

3.6.2   Advertisements

The Tenant must not fix to or exhibit on the outside of the Premises, or fix to or exhibit through any window of the Premises, or display anywhere on the Premises any placard, sign, notice, fascia, board or advertisement, except, with the consent of the Landlord such consent not to be unreasonably withheld or delayed, a sign of the same design, so far as possible, as those the Tenant has the right, by virtue of Schedule 2 clause 3 DISPLAY OF NAMEPLATES OR SIGNS, to have displayed on the outside of the Building and in the reception area of the Building PROVIDED ALWAYS that nothing in this subclause or in any other provision of this Lease shall preclude the Tenant from displaying its usual trade or corporate logo as aforesaid

3.7   *Statutory obligations*

3.7.1   General provision

To the extent that compliance is not the obligation of the Landlord pursuant to his obligations contained in this Lease or under the general law and save where the same involves capital expenditure or in respect of an inherent Defect the Tenant must comply in all respects with the requirements of any statutes applicable to the use by the Tenant of the Premises or the trade or business for the time being carried on there and any other obligations so applicable imposed by law or by any byelaws

3.7.2   Particular obligations

3.5.4   This amendment is simply designed to translate an absolute prohibition into a qualified prohibition. There are often no compelling reasons at the outset of a transaction why there should be an absolute prohibition on the tenant from doing certain things on the premises which will not adversely affect the value of the landlord's reversion. A qualified prohibition will almost always give the landlord the necessary protection because if what is proposed is likely to damage the value of his reversion or, in any other way, cause him difficulty he is entitled to refuse consent. An absolute prohibition, on the other hand from the tenant's perspective, gives the tenant absolutely no room for manoeuvre and should, when appropriate, be strenuously resisted.

3.6.1   Exactly the same point can be made here as under **clause 3.5.4.** The extension to the list of hardware items simply reflects changing technology.

3.6.2   The first amendment again changes the obligation from an absolute prohibition to a qualified prohibition while the proviso at the end of the clause provides that any nationally recognised or instantly recognisable trade or corporate logos are not subject to any such control. If the landlord has been negotiating to grant a lease to a party who has such trade logos it is reasonably safe to assume that part of the attraction from the landlord's point of view is likely to be the strength of the covenant associated with that body.

3.7.1   The first amendment ensures that liability for compliance is accepted by the landlord where either he has freely accepted it in the lease or by virtue of the general law, while the words in brackets should be included in a shorter-term lease to ensure the tenant is not paying to improve the value of the landlord's investment or where the work is required to repair an inherent defect (as defined) in case the tenant is not responsible for inherent defects but nor has the landlord assumed responsibility for these. If this amendment is made a consequential amendment will be necessary to the landlord's covenants so that the landlord is liable for compliance with these issues as otherwise there may be a lacuna with neither the landlord or tenant liable. In addition, the tenant's adviser should ensure the landlord cannot recover any expenditure it incurs via the service charge (see para 2.3 of Schedule 6). The second amendment pro-

posed here attempts to narrow down the tenant's liability so that it is only the tenant's actual presence and use of the building which gives rise to an obligation to comply with the statutes referred to. So far as the building itself is concerned, particularly in relation to shorter-term lettings, this clause as drafted is an attempt by the landlord to shift the responsibility for compliance to the tenant. The amendment seeks to shift it back!

One new piece of legislation whose impact the tenant needs to consider is the Disability Discrimination Act 1995. Part III of the Disability Discrimination Act 1995 places duties on those providing goods, facilities and services (known as 'service providers') not to discriminate against disabled people. Since 2 December 1996, it has been unlawful for service providers to treat people with a disability any less favourably for any reason relating to their disability. Since the beginning of October 1999, service providers have been under a statutory duty to make *reasonable adjustments* where it is impossible or unreasonably difficult for disabled people to make use of any service they provide. From 2004 onwards, a statutory duty exists on service providers to make *reasonable adjustments* to any physical features of their premises to overcome physical barriers to access. There are legal and political reasons why tenants in non-compliant buildings need now to start planning ahead for the future, and take whatever steps may be necessary to comply with the statutory duties that are currently in force, and to plan ahead in relation to physical features of buildings they occupy. A failure to do so now could lead to costly court actions being taken against those service providers, with the distinct possibility of both damages being awarded and an order made requiring compliance with these duties.

A code of practice is currently available from the Stationery Office, giving practical guidance on Part III of the Disability Discrimination Act 1995. The duty is not limited to tenants, because both landlords and tenants can be seen as being service providers. A good example would be a shopping centre or a multi-let building where common parts are provided. It is important that all parties involved in commercial lease negotiation plan ahead to ensure that they are taking such steps as are reasonable in the circumstances to remove any physical features which might make it impossible or unreasonably difficult for a disabled person to use any such service, or to alter it in such a way that it does not cause a difficulty, or to ensure they provide reasonable means of avoiding the feature. Clearly, specific advice needs to be taken in relation to any particular building, and any particular potential physical feature. However, with the impending consequences of this Act, tenants, in particular, need to be aware and to ensure that some form of audit is done prior to finalising the lease, so that if there are any cost implications in relation to compliance, this can be factored into the overall deal it agrees with the landlord on the terms of the lease.

3.7.2.1   Works required by statute, department or authority

Without prejudice to the generality of clause 3.7.1, the Tenant must execute all works and provide and maintain all arrangements on or in respect of ~~the Premises or~~ the use to which the Premises are being put that are required in order to comply with the requirements of any statute already ~~or in the future to be~~ passed, or the requirements of any government department, local authority or other public or competent authority or court of competent jurisdiction~~, regardless of whether such requirements are imposed on the owner, the occupier, or any other person~~ <u>unless compliance with the same is within the responsibility of the Landlord pursuant to the terms of this Lease</u>

3.7.2.2   Acts causing losses

Without prejudice to the generality of clause 3.7.1, the Tenant must not <u>knowingly</u> do in or near the Premises anything by reason of which the Landlord may incur any losses under any statute

3.7.2.3   Construction (Design and Management) Regulations

Without prejudice to the generality of clause 3.7.1, the Tenant must <u>insofar as they relate to any works the tenant may undertake</u> comply with the provisions of the Construction (Design and Management) Regulations 1994 ('the CDM Regulations'), be the only client as defined in the provisions of the CDM Regulations, fulfil in relation to all and any works all the obligations of the client as set out in or reasonably to be inferred from the CDM Regulations, and make a declaration to that effect to the Health and Safety Executive in accordance with the Approved Code of Practice published from time to time by the Health and Safety Executive in relation to the CDM Regulations. The provisions of clause 5.7.3 FIREFIGHTING EQUIPMENT are to have effect in any circumstances to which these obligations apply

3.7.2.4   Delivery of health and safety files

At the end of the Term, the Tenant must ~~forthwith~~ <u>as soon as reasonably practicable</u> deliver to the Landlord any and all health and safety files relating to the premises in accordance with the CDM Regulations

3.8   *Entry to inspect and notice to repair*

3.8.1   Entry and notice

<u>Where the same cannot otherwise be undertaken</u> ~~T~~the Tenant must permit the Landlord <u>(on reasonable prior written notice)</u>

3.7.2.1   The first deletion in this particular clause merely attempts to reinforce the points made under **clause 3.7.1** while the second attempts
to ensure that the *extent* of the tenant's liability is fixed at the date
of the lease and not extended by subsequent statutes or subordinate
legislation. The final deletion seeks to reinforce the first of these
points. The tenant needs to give some thought as to the possible
implications of this clause in the context of contamination. The
author is of the view that it will and the tenant must take steps to
safeguard itself. If thought necessary an environmental audit can be
an efficient insurance policy. The additional words at the end of the
clause seek to shift responsibility back to the landlord for environmental compliance (see new **clause 4.6**).

3.7.2.2   This clause imposes *strict liability* on the part of the tenant, and the
tenant's adviser should try to introduce the element of knowledge
and seek to ensure that his client is not unknowingly saddled with
this liability. It is, in reality, very likely to be impossible to comply at
all times during a lease term with all relevant statutes which relate
to occupation of a building and few, if any, tenants are going to
know the full extent of their statutory obligations.

3.7.2.3   The Construction (Design and Management) Regulations 1994
apply in only a limited set of circumstances and in relation to particular works of construction and the detail is beyond the scope of
this book. There is one argument for stating that this clause should
be deleted in its entirety bearing in mind the wide provisions contained in **clause 3.7.1** but the amendment here makes the provisions operative only in so far as they relate to any works the tenant
may decide to undertake.

3.7.2.4   An obligation to do something *forthwith* is, in many circumstances,
likely to prove impossible to comply with. The proposed amendment simply attempts to deal with the reality of this situation.

3.8.1   The proposed amendment to this clause seeks to ensure that before
entering the premises occupied by the tenant (and causing disruption and possible alarm amongst the tenant's employees 'Why were
the landlord's representatives crawling around the office yester-

or during normal business hours except in emergency or by appointment if the Tenant makes such an appointment within a reasonable time following the Landlord's notice:

3.8.1.1   to enter the Premises to ascertain whether or not the covenants and conditions of this Lease have been observed and performed,

3.8.1.2   to view the state of repair and condition of the Premises and other parts of the Premises where that is necessary in order to do so the Landlord making good as soon as reasonably practicable any damage thereby caused when such opening up reveals no breaches, and

3.8.1.3   to give to the Tenant, or notwithstanding clause 8.6 NOTICES leave on the Premises, a notice ('a notice to repair') specifying the works required to remedy any breach of the Tenant's obligations in this Lease which has caused or is likely to cause substantial damage to or dimunition in the value of the Landlord's reversion

3.8.2   Works to be carried out

The Tenant must commence carrying out the works specified in a notice to repair as soon as reasonably practicable immediately, (including, making good any opening up) (but only where the opening up has revealed breaches)

3.8.3   Landlord's power in default

If within 1 month of the service of a notice to repair the Tenant has not started to execute the work referred to in that notice or is not proceeding diligently with it, or if the Tenant fails to finish the work as soon as reasonably practicable within 2 months or if in the Landlord's reasonable opinion the Tenant is unlikely to finish the work within the reasonable period, the Tenant must permit the Landlord to enter the Premises to execute the outstanding work, and must, on demand, pay to the Landlord the reasonable and proper cost of so doing and all expenses incurred by the Landlord, including legal costs and surveyor's fees as soon as reasonably practicable PROVIDED ALWAYS that any such costs which fall to be reimbursed by the Tenant shall not exceed any which would be recoverable by the Landlord pursuant to the relevant provisions of the Leasehold Property (Repairs) Act 1938 and section 18(1) of the Landlord and Tenant Act 1927 and PROVIDED FURTHER (and for the avoidance of doubt) the execution of such works by the Landlord shall not be deemed to exclude the provisions of either statute referred to in this sub-clause

day?') the landlord has explored whether or not there is any alternative available to him before coming onto the premises. If this is absolutely necessary there should at least be some reasonable notice in order that the tenant can take the appropriate action, ie arrange for this to be done outside office hours or notifying staff that there is nothing to worry about and what the purpose of the inspection is.

3.8.1.2   Opening up floors could cause untold problems for a tenant and this should be forcibly resisted. If a landlord insists then he must accept that if the opening up reveals no breaches of covenant not only should he make good any physical damage he may have caused to the premises but, if the tenant has suffered any financial loss, this too should be made good by the landlord. The risks associated may well serve as sufficient deterrent to the landlord. The amendment suggested achieves this.

3.8.1.3   The suggested amendment will prevent the landlord serving a notice for relatively minor breaches, such as a breach of the covenant to decorate in a specified year. It will provide a useful check on the landlord in these circumstances.

3.8.2   The first two amendments here are self-explanatory and seek to give a tenant a little more scope as regards a timetable for commencing any necessary works while the final amendment seeks to ensure that if the landlord has opened up any part of the premises (which the tenant should most definitely try and resist) and no breaches have been revealed then the obligation to reinstate rests with the landlord and not the tenant.

3.8.3   The landlord's self-help remedy contained in this clause is not available unless specifically set out and therefore, ideally, the tenant's adviser should delete it! The clause has the effect of allowing the landlord to recover the costs of such works as a debt and it has the benefit (from the landlord's point of view) of avoiding the provisions of the Leasehold Property (Repairs) Act 1938 because the landlord's claim is for a debt and not damages. In addition and for the same reason the limitation imposed on the level of recoverable costs by section 18(1) of the Landlord and Tenant Act 1927 will not apply. These principles were confirmed in *Jervis v Harris* [1996] 1 All ER 303, CA but were qualified in their application in *London Borough of Hammersmith & Fulham v Creska* [1999] P&CR D46 where the court declined to allow the landlord an injunction (an equitable remedy) to enter premises to carry out repairs on the ground that damages were an adequate remedy. If the tenant does not succeed in having the clause deleted the amendments to the clause seek to ensure that the balance is as fair as possible in relation to works which are required. As the provision only operates when the tenant is in default a landlord will seek to argue that there should be no fetter on the costs that he incurs in exercising his self-help remedy but the tenant will be ill advised to accept an obligation effectively to present the landlord with a blank cheque. The proviso attempts to contractually incorporate the statutory provisions and nullify the clause's attempt to 'contract-out' of them.

3.8.4   Exempt information documentation application

If the Landlord provides to the Tenant completed forms EX1 and EX1A within [7 days] of the date of this Lease together with a cheque for the relevant fee, the Tenant must submit simultaneously with any application to HM Land Registry for first registration of this Lease any applications in forms EX1 and EX1A that the Landlord [reasonably] requires

3.9   *Alienation*

3.9.1   Alienation prohibited

The Tenant must not hold the Premises on trust for another. The Tenant must not part with possession of the Premises or any part of them or permit another to occupy them or any part of them except pursuant to a transaction permitted by and effected in accordance with the provisions of this Lease

3.9.2   Assignment, ~~subletting~~ and charging of part |

The Tenant must not assign, ~~sublet~~ or charge part only of the |
Premises.

3.9.3   Assignment of the whole

Subject to clauses 3.9.4 CIRCUMSTANCES and 3.9.5 CONDI-TIONS, the Tenant must not assign the whole of the Premises without the consent of the Landlord, whose consent may not be unreasonably withheld or delayed |

Does the landlord or tenant want to keep certain information out of the public domain? The general rule is that all registers at the Land Registry are open for public inspection, other than an exempt information document, so that anyone can apply for an official copy of the entries in the register of title, the title plan, documents referred to in the register and also any other documents held by the Registrar which relate to an application to him. This, it should be noted, includes leases. However, it is possible to apply to the Registrar for the lease to be designated as an exempt information document if it is claimed that the lease contains prejudicial information. Prejudicial information is defined as information that relates to an individual who is the applicant which, if disclosed to other persons (whether to the public generally or specific persons), would, or would be likely to, cause substantial unwarranted distress to the applicant or another, or information which, if disclosed to other persons (whether to the public generally or specific persons), would, or would be likely to, prejudice the commercial interests of the applicant for exemption. Despite this there is a procedure by which a person may apply for an official copy of an exempt information document if he considers that the omitted information is not prejudicial information.

3.9   ***Recommendation 9 of the Code: Assigning and subletting:***
Unless the particular circumstances of the letting justify greater control, the only restriction on assignment of the whole premises should be obtaining the landlord's consent which is not to be unreasonably withheld. Landlords are urged to consider requiring Authorised Guarantee Agreements only where the assignee is of lower financial standing than the assignor at the date of the assignment.

3.9.2   While stating the obvious that the tenant's adviser must always look at the particular circumstances of the letting and the needs of the tenant, the letting envisaged by our specimen lease is a classic example where there is likely to be merit in the tenant having the ability to sublet *part* of the premises. As the premises are arranged on three different levels it may well be possible to agree with the landlord, as a point of principle, that subletting either the whole of a particular floor or specified parts of each floor should be acceptable to the landlord. The amendment proposed seeks to cater for that eventuality.

3.9.3   There is a vast legal difference between *withholding* and *delaying* consents and while a tenant has statutory rights in such circumstances under the Landlord and Tenant Act 1988, the additional words seek to reinforce the statutory provisions that the tenant has redress in damages for breach of statutory duty if the landlord delays.

3.9.4 Circumstances

If any of the following circumstances (which are specified for the purposes of the Landlord and Tenant Act 1927 section 19(1A)) applies either at the date when application for consent to assign is made to the Landlord, or after that date but before the Landlord's consent is given, the Landlord may withhold his consent and if, after the Landlord's consent has been given but before the assignment has taken place, any such circumstances apply, the Landlord may revoke his consent, ~~whether~~ where his consent is expressly subject to a condition as referred to in subclause 3.9.5.4 ~~or not~~. The circumstances are:

3.9.4.1 that any <u>undisputed and material</u> sum due from the Tenant under this Lease remains unpaid

3.9.4.2 that in the Landlord's reasonable opinion the assignee is not a person who is likely to be able to comply with the tenant covenants of this Lease ~~and to continue to be able to comply with them following the assignment~~

3.9.4.3 that without prejudice to subclause 3.9.4.2, in the case of an assignment to a Group Company in the Landlord's reasonable opinion the assignee is a person who is, or may become, less likely to be able to comply with the tenant covenants of this Lease than the Tenant requesting consent to assign, which likelihood is to be adjudged by reference in particular to the financial strength of that Tenant ~~aggregated with that of any guarantor of the obligations of that Tenant~~ and the value of any other security for the performance of the tenant covenants of this Lease when assessed at the date of grant or (where that Tenant is not the Original Tenant) the date of the assignment of this Lease to that Tenant or

3.9.4.4 that the assignee or any guarantor for the assignee, other than any guarantor under an authorised guarantee agreement, is a corporation registered (or otherwise resident) in a jurisdiction in which the order of a court obtained in England and Wales will not necessarily be enforced against the assignee or guarantor without any consideration of the merits of the case

3.9.5 Conditions

The Landlord may impose any or all of the following conditions which are specified for the purposes of the Landlord and Tenant Act 1927 section 19(1A) on giving any consent for an assignment by the Tenant, and any such consent is to be treated as being subject to each of the following:

3.9.5.1 a condition that <u>if reasonably so required by the Landlord</u> on or before any assignment and before giving occupation to the assignee, the Tenant requesting consent to assign, together

3.9.4   This amendment is self-explanatory.

Recommendation 16 of the Code: Holding former tenants and their guarantors liable: When previous tenants or their guarantors are liable to a landlord for defaults by the current tenant, landlords should notify them before the current tenant accumulates excessive liabilities. All defaults should be handled with speed and landlords should seek to assist the tenant and guarantor in minimising losses. An assignor who wishes to remain informed of the outcome of rent reviews should keep in touch with the landlord and the landlord should provide the information. Assignors should take professional advice on what methods are open to them to minimise their losses caused by defaults by the current occupier.

3.9.4.1   It may be that, at the time an application is made for the relevant licence to assign, a sum of money allegedly due from tenant to landlord is unpaid but the reason that it has not been paid by the tenant is that it is disputed. If there is a genuine dispute there is no reason why this should delay landlord's consent. In addition insignificant outstanding sums should not delay the giving of consent.

3.9.4.2   The words which have been deleted here are very difficult to interpret, smack of crystal ball gazing and act in a most unfair way against the tenant and any possible assignee. There is always a possibility that at some time in the future an assignee is not going to be able to comply with the tenant's covenants in the lease irrespective of its initial covenant strength. Nothing in the future is *absolutely* guaranteed. The judgement as to whether an assignee is likely to be able to *currently* comply has to be made by the landlord at the time the application for consent is made. (See *Ashworth Frazer Ltd v Gloucester City Council* [2001] UKHL 59, [2002] 1 All ER 377.)

3.9.4.3   The amendment here simply seeks to compare like with like. It will often be the case that the covenant strength of an original tenant aggregated with that of a guarantor is going to be greater than that of a potential assignee alone if only because it gives the landlord two parties against whom to take action. The tenant's adviser should seek to make the deletion suggested.

3.9.5.1   The Code (recommendation 9) urges landlords to require an authorised guarantee agreement only where the assignee is of lower financial standing than the assignor at the date of assignment. This

with any former tenant who by virtue of the 1995 Act section 11 was not released on an earlier assignment of this Lease, must enter into an authorised guarantee agreement in favour of the Landlord in the terms set out in Schedule 8 THE AUTHO-RISED GUARANTEE AGREEMENT

3.9.5.2   a condition that if reasonably so required by the Landlord on an assignment to a limited company, the assignee must ensure that at least 2 directors of the company, or some other guarantor or guarantors <u>reasonably</u> acceptable to the Landlord, enter into direct covenants with the Landlord in the form of the guarantor's covenants contained in clause 6 GUARANTEE PROVISIONS with 'the Assignee' substituted for 'the Tenant'

3.9.5.3   a condition that upon or before any assignment, the Tenant making the request for consent to assign must <u>if applicable in the particular circumstances of the proposed assignment</u> give to the Landlord a copy of the health and safety file required to be maintained under the Construction (Design and Management) Regulations 1994 containing full details of all works undertaken to the Premises by that Tenant and

3.9.5.4   a condition that if, at any time before the assignment, the cir-cumstances specified in clause 3.9.4, or any of them, apply, the Landlord may revoke the consent by written notice to the Tenant <u>with written reasons therefore</u>

3.9.6   Charging of the whole

The Tenant must not charge the whole of the Premises without the consent of the Landlord, whose consent may not be unrea-sonably withheld or delayed <u>PROVIDED ALWAYS that this clause is not to prevent the creation of a floating charge over all the assets of the Tenant for the purposes of his normal banking arrangements and the existence of any charge creat-ed by him for such purposes over acquired property at the date on which his interest in the Premises arose does not con-stitute a breach of this subclause</u>

3.9.7   Subletting

The Tenant must not sublet the whole <u>or a Permitted Part</u> of the Premises without the consent of the Landlord, whose consent may not be unreasonably withheld <u>or delayed</u>

3.9.8   Terms of a permitted sublease

Every permitted sublease must be granted, without a fine or premium, at a rent not less than ~~whichever is the greater of~~ the then open market rent payable in respect of the Premises to be approved by the Landlord before the sublease and to be deter-

amendment reflects that recommendation. In *Wallis Fashion Group Ltd v CGU Life Assurance Ltd* [2000] 2 EGLR 49 on lease renewal the court held that the landlord could only insist on the new lease containing a requirement of an authorised guarantee agreement from the tenant if reasonably required.

3.9.5.2   If the landlord reasonably requires a guarantee from at least two directors of the assignee company, it will be in the interests of the tenant to have this guarantee as the tenant will remain liable to pay the rent and comply with the lease covenants after the assignment if he was, as is very likely, required to enter into an authorised guarantee agreement.

3.9.5.3   The amendment is self-explanatory and seeks to make consideration by a landlord a wholly subjective one.

3.9.5.4   The proposed amendment seeks to give the tenant something against which to argue and reflects the landlord's obligation under the Landlord and Tenant Act 1988. If a tenant has detailed written reasons at least issue can be taken if the tenant or assignee disagrees.

3.9.6   Ideally the tenant should seek to delete this clause in its entirety but a landlord is unlikely to accept this. The primary reason for the deletion is that any financial institution taking a charge over the lease is most likely to have a greater covenant strength than that of the tenant and in theory, therefore, if that chargee enforced its security and took possession the landlord would be in a better position. However landlords are likely to be very suspicious about this and its deletion is not likely to prove acceptable. The proviso which has been added seeks to ensure that the granting of debentures which affect the entirety of any corporate tenant's property portfolio is not prevented. It is unlikely, in the author's view, that a landlord would find this proviso unacceptable.

3.9.7   This amendment reflects and follows through the suggested amendment under **clause 3.9.2**. As to the definition of a 'permitted Part' see **clause 1.33** and the note on this clause.

3.9.8   In recent recessionary times with falling rents it was often impossible for tenants to sublet either a part or the whole of the premises because of the existence of a clause such as the one originally drafted here. If rents have fallen and the open market rent is in fact less than the passing rent it is going to be difficult, if not impossible, for a tenant to find a subtenant prepared to pay the passing rent. No properly advised prospective subtenant would accept this, especially in view of the Court of Appeal decision in *Allied Dunbar Assurance*

mined by the Surveyor, acting as an expert and not as an arbi-trator and such Rent, to be payable in advance on the days on which the Rent is payable under this Lease. Every permitted sublease must contain provisions approved by the Landlord:

3.9.8.1   for the upwards only review of the rent reserved by it, on the basis set out in Schedule 4 THE RENT AND RENT REVIEW and on the Review Dates

3.9.8.2   prohibiting the subtenant from doing or allowing anything in relation to the Premises inconsistent with or in breach of the provisions of this Lease

3.9.8.3   for re-entry by the sublandlord on breach of any covenant by the subtenant

3.9.8.4   imposing an absolute prohibition against all dealings with the Premises other than assignment or subletting of the whole or a Permitted Part

3.9.8.5   prohibiting assignment or subletting of the whole or a Permitted Part of the Premises without the prior consent of the Landlord under this Lease

3.9.8.6   requiring the assignee on any assignment of the sublease to enter into direct covenants with the Landlord to the same effect as those contained in clause 3.9.9 SUBTENANT'S DIRECT COVENANTS

3.9.8.7   requiring on each assignment of the sublease that the assign-or enters into an authorised guarantee agreement in favour of the Landlord in the terms set out in Schedule 8 THE AUTHO-RISED GUARANTEE AGREEMENT but adapted to suit the cir-cumstances in which the guarantee is given

3.9.8.8   prohibiting the subtenant from holding on trust for another or permitting another to share or occupy the whole or any part of the Premises

plc v Homebase Ltd [2002] EWCA Civ 666, [2003] IP&CR 75, where it was decided that the landlord could refuse consent if there was a subletting which complied with the covenant but was accompanied by a side letter and collateral agreement which varied this. It is, therefore, only fair that a tenant should have the ability to sublet at what is an open market rent in order to subsidise his over-rented premises. Landlords are in practice not likely to be in a worse position and any concerns of the landlord can be met if any such sublease is *'contracted out'*. Landlords still have the benefit of the original tenant covenant (and possibly a guarantor) and can insist on an open market rent review in the sublease. Any concern a landlord expresses that he may be stuck with a lower passing rent should he forfeit the head lease is unfounded. If the head lease is forfeited, a subtenant can apply for relief against forfeiture (by virtue of an application for a vesting order) but relief from forfeiture is most likely to be granted to a subtenant at a rental equivalent to the old head lease rent (apportioned if the sublease applies to only part of the premises comprised in the old head lease) although the courts do retain a discretion to fix a 'fair rent' (*London Bridge Buildings Co v Thomson* (1903) 89 LT 50). An additional reason for making this change can be found by referring to the BFP initiative explained in the note on the Code at the front of this book following the Code itself.

The courts held in *NCR Ltd v Riverland Portfolio No 1 Ltd* [2004] 16 EG 110 that the payment of a reverse premium to a prospective underlessee was not caught by the decision in *Allied Dunbar* referred to above.

3.9.8.4 and 3.9.8.5   This ties in with the amendment introduced into the definitions section under **clause 1.33 (new)** which defined a *Permitted Part* in relation to which a sublease can be granted.

3.9.8.11   For management reasons the landlord may wish to ensure that any subtenants do not obtain security of tenure. It will in practice be a question of the bargaining strength of the parties as to whose view will prevail. The author has deleted the subclause on the basis that it is up to the landlord to come up with compelling reasons as to why security of tenure should be excluded from the proposed subletting. The landlord may have genuine concerns if the covenant of the underlessee is weaker than that of the tenant and in consequence a good reason for withholding his consent to an underletting (see *NCR Ltd v Riverland Properties No 1 Ltd* [2004] 16 EG 110). Also in the case of an underletting of a permitted part the landlord may well have genuine concerns that an unsatisfactory subdivision may be perpetuated and the value of his reversion diminished, unless the security provisions the Landlord and Tenant Act 1954 are excluded. Of course the tenant itself may at the time of the subletting wish to exclude the securing provisions for its own benefit in order to reoccupy and then renew the lease of the entire premises on its expiry or

3.9.8.9   imposing in relation to any permitted assignment or subletting the same obligations for registration with the Landlord as are contained in this Lease in relation to dispositions by the Tenant

3.9.8.10   imposing in relation to any permitted subletting the same obligations as are contained in this clause 3.9.8 and in clauses 3.9.9 SUBTENANT'S DIRECT COVENANTS, 3.9.10 ENFORCEMENT ETC OF SUBLEASES and 3.9.11 SUBLEASE RENT REVIEW and

3.9.8.11   ~~excluding the provisions of sections 24-28 of the 1954 Act from the letting created by the sublease~~

3.9.9   Subtenant's direct covenants

Before any permitted subletting, the Tenant must ensure that the subtenant enters into a direct covenant with the Landlord that while the subtenant is bound by the tenant covenants of the sublease and while he is bound by an authorised guarantee agreement the subtenant will observe and perform the tenant covenants contained in this Lease except the covenant to pay the rent reserved by this Lease and in that sublease.

3.9.10   ~~Requirement for an exclusion order~~

~~The Tenant must not grant a sublease or permit a subtenant to occupy the Premises unless an order has been obtained under section 38(4) of the 1954 Act.~~

3.9.10   Enforcement, waiver and variation of subleases

The Tenant must enforce the performance and observance by the subtenant of the provisions of every permitted sublease, and must not at any time either expressly or by implication knowingly waive any breach of the covenants or conditions on the part of any subtenant or assignee of any sublease, or (without the consent of the Landlord whose consent is not to be unreasonably withheld or delayed) vary the terms or accept a surrender of any permitted sublease.

3.9.11   Sublease rent review

In relation to any permitted sublease:

3.9.11.1   the Tenant must ensure that the rent is reviewed in accordance with the terms of the sublease

3.9.11.2   the Tenant must not agree the reviewed rent with the subtenant without the approval of the Landlord such approval not to be unreasonably withheld or delayed

claim compensation for the whole of the premises. If the landlord has the contractual right to refuse a proposed subtenant on the basis of covenant strength, there is a question mark over any argument he puts forward arguing against security of tenure for a covenant which by agreeing to the subletting in the first place satisfies its own tests (see **clause 3.5.8**).

3.9.10 (deleted) This is simply a belt and braces provision for the landlord in relation to the *contracting out* of any sublease. As mentioned above in relation to **clause 3.9.8.11** it is a question of the relative bargaining strength of the parties as to whose arguments will win the day. In theory at least the requirement that any subtenancy be subject to an exclusion order may make subletting that bit more difficult for the tenant in an already difficult marketplace.

3.9.10 (new) The amendments here are self-explanatory (see **clauses 3.5.4** and **3.7.2.2**). The tenant, as the subtenant's landlord, cannot be expected to police the premises every single day and is only likely to become aware of a breach by the subtenant when something goes wrong. Hence the addition of the word '*knowingly*'. The second amendment imposes an obligation on the landlord to act reasonably and no such statutory implication exists in these circumstances.

3.9.11.2 This amendment provides that when deciding whether or not to agree to the reviewed rent with the subtenant, the head landlord is

3.9.11.3 where the sublease provides such an option, the Tenant must not, without the approval of the Landlord such approval not to be unreasonably withheld or delayed, agree whether the third party determining the revised rent in default of agreement should act as an arbitrator or as an expert

3.9.11.4 the Tenant must not, without the approval of the Landlord such approval not to be unreasonably withheld or delayed, agree any appointment of a person to act as the third party determining the revised rent

3.9.11.5 the Tenant must incorporate as part of his representations to that third party representations reasonably required by the Landlord and

3.9.11.6 the Tenant must give notice to the Landlord of the details of the determination of every rent review within 28 days

3.9.12   Registration and notification of dealings and occupation

3.9.12.1 In this clause a **Transaction** is:

(a)   any dealing with this lease or the devolution or transmission of, or parting with possession of any interest in it; or

(b)   the creation of any underlease or other interest out of this lease, or out of any interest, underlease derived from it, and any dealing, devolution or transmission of, or parting with possession of any such interest or underlease; or

(c)   the making of any other arrangement for the occupation of the Property

3.9.12.2 In respect of every Transaction that is registrable at HM Land Registry, the Tenant shall promptly following completion of the Transaction use all reasonable endeavours to apply to register it (or procure that the relevant person so applies). The Tenant shall use all reasonable endeavours (or shall procure that) any requisitions raised by HM Land Registry in connection with an application to register a Transaction are dealt with promptly and properly. Within one month of completion of the registration, the Tenant shall send the Landlord official copies of its title (and where applicable of the undertenant's title).

3.9.12.3 No later than one month after a Transaction the Tenant shall:

(a)   give the Landlord's solicitors notice of the Transaction; and

under a contractual obligation to behave reasonably. Again no such statutory obligation exists in such circumstances and such a requirement must be spelt out.

3.9.11.3   See the comments under **clause 3.9.11.2** above.

3.9.11.4   See the comments under **clause 3.9.11.2** above.

3.9.11.5   See the comments under **clause 3.9.11.2** above.

3.9.12   The amendment here is designed to give certainty. Like everything else within the confines of a commercial lease, many landlords are increasingly seeking to impose the cost of any involvement they have in the management of the premises on the tenant and the tenant will often consider such charges to be unreasonable. Deletion of the words '*at least*' gives a fixed fee liability and prevents the tenant from being at the mercy of his landlord.

3.9.13 (new)   Any corporate tenant that is a member (or indeed likely to become a member) of a wider group should insist upon a provision being incorporated in a lease which gives maximum flexibility in terms of occupation with other group companies. A landlord would normally find such a group sharing clause acceptable but may add a further proviso to the effect that such sharing would be acceptable only for so long as the two companies remain members of the same group (see **clause 1.11**) *and* in so far as the sharing of occupation does not give rise to a new tenancy between those two companies. This is an acceptable compromise in the author's view. It may also be worth trying to amend the group sharing clause shown to include any franchises or concessionaires who may wish to share occupation on similar terms to that of a group company or in some cases no interest greater than a tenancy at will, which will allow a member of the Group (while it remains within the same relationship) to enjoy exclusive possession, but not to acquire security under the Landlord & Tenant Act 1954.

3.10.1   As originally drafted this clause is vague, incapable of legal certainty and very subjective. What is one person's annoyance is another

(b)   deliver two certified copies of any document effecting the Transaction to the Landlord's solicitors and

(c)   pay the Landlord's solicitors a registration fee of £30 (plus VAT)

3.9.12.4 If the Landlord so <u>reasonably</u> requests, the Tenant shall |
promptly supply the Landlord with full details of the occupiers of the Property and the terms upon which they occupy it

3.9.13   <u>Sharing with a Group Company</u>

<u>Notwithstanding clause 3.9.1 ALIENATION PROHIBITED, the Tenant may share the occupation of the whole or any part of the Premises with a Group Company or grant a tenancy at will to a Group Company</u> |

3.10   Closure of the Registered Title of this Lease

Immediately after the end of the term (and notwithstanding that the term has ended), the Tenant shall make an application to close the registered title of this lease and shall <u>use all rea-</u> |
<u>sonable endeavours</u> to ensure that any requisitions raised by |
HM Land Registry in connection with that application are dealt with promptly and properly, the Tenant shall keep the Landlord informed of the progress and completion of its application.

3.11   *Nuisance and residential restrictions*

3.11.1   Nuisance

The Tenant must not do anything on the Premises or allow anything to remain on them that may be or become or cause a <u>legal</u> nuisance, or annoyance, disturbance, inconvenience, |
injury or damage to the Landlord or his tenants or the owners or occupiers of adjacent or neighbouring premises <u>PROVIDED</u> |
<u>ALWAYS that the proper use of the Premises as offices by the Tenant shall not in any circumstances constitute a breach of this obligation and PROVIDED FURTHER that nothing in this</u> |
<u>sub-clause [or elsewhere in this Lease] shall oblige the Tenant to be responsible for compliance with any environmental statutes, regulations and orders</u>

person's pleasure. Annoyance, disturbance and inconvenience have no foundation in law as they are not recognised torts. The amendment seeks to ensure that what can and cannot be done by the tenant is set against some proper legal barometer. The proviso added is self-explanatory but is an important addition to give the tenant peace of mind in using the premises for the permitted use set out in paragraph 1.1 of Schedule 5. The landlord will have taken into account the tenant's proposed use of the premises at the time it decided either to grant the lease or consent to the assignment and this should be sufficient to ensure that the tenant's proper use of the offices does not constitute a breach of this clause. The further proviso added at the end once again attempts to deal with the issue of contamination. For a comprehensive clause relieving the tenant from liability for historic contamination see Precedent 30 in Division R of Ross: Commercial Leases.

3.10.2 The author has added a similar proviso at the end of this clause for the same reason as that stated at **clause 3.10.1**. For many years the author tried to ascertain why the antiquated notion of banning auctions existed. Finding little to help in texts he was grateful to a practitioner who explained that landlords were simply concerned that a '... a mass of people stampeding at an auction was likely to damage the fabric of the premises, something a landlord wanted to avoid!'. Readers will draw their own conclusion as to whether references to auctions should remain!

3.11 The addition of the words *reasonable and proper* shown in the text in substitution for the deleted words is, in the author's view, still sufficient protection for the landlord. If the landlord has incurred unreasonable or improper charges then there is no reason why, on the indemnity basis originally sought, a tenant should be liable for these and hence the deletion. Not only should the costs be 'reasonable and proper' costs, but they should also be 'reasonably and properly' incurred. Hence the second amendment.

3.11.1 If the landlord behaves unlawfully or unreasonably in withholding or delaying consent or offers the consent subject to unlawful or unreasonable conditions or qualifications, there is no reason why a tenant should be responsible for reimbursing the costs that the landlord has incurred in coming to this unsustainable conclusion. All that the tenant is asking the landlord to do is to conduct himself in a manner consistent with both his statutory and contractual obligations. If the landlord's behaviour is inconsistent with these obligations then he must take account of the possible cost implications and also appreciate that the tenant may pursue a claim against him for damages under the Landlord and Tenant Act 1988 if consent is sought for an assignment or underletting of the premises.

3.11.2   Auctions, trades and immoral purposes

The Tenant must not use the Premises for a sale by auction or for any dangerous, noxious, noisy or offensive trade, business, manufacture or occupation, or any illegal or immoral act or purpose PROVIDED ALWAYS that the proper use of the Premises as offices by the Tenant shall not in any circumstances constitute a breach of this obligation

3.11.3   Residential use, sleeping and animals

The Tenant must not use the Premises as sleeping accommodation or for residential purposes, or keep any animal on them

3.11.4   Costs of applications, notices and recovery of arrears

The Tenant must pay to the Landlord ~~on an indemnity basis~~ all reasonable and proper costs, fees, charges, disbursements and expenses (including without prejudice to the generality of the above those payable to counsel, solicitors, surveyors and bailiffs) reasonably and properly incurred by the Landlord in relation to or incidental to:

3.11.5   every application made by the Tenant for a consent or licence required by the provisions of this Lease~~, whether it is granted, refused or offered subject to any qualification or condition, or the application is withdrawn~~ unless the same is unlawfully or unreasonably withheld or delayed or offered subject to some unlawful or unreasonable condition

3.11.6   the lawful and proper ~~contemplation or~~ preparation and service of a notice under the Law of Property Act 1925, section 146, or by reason of the lawful and proper ~~contemplation or~~ taking of proceedings under sections 146 or 147 of that Act, even if forfeiture is avoided otherwise than by relief granted by the court

3.11.7   the recovery or attempted recovery of arrears of rent or other sums due under this Lease and

3.11.8   any lawful and proper steps taken in ~~contemplation~~ direct connection with the preparation and service of a schedule of dilapidations during or within six months after the end of the Term but only in relation to any dilapidations occurring during the Term

3.12   *Planning and development*

3.12.1   Compliance with the Planning Acts

The Tenant must observe and comply with the provisions and requirements of the Planning Acts affecting the Premises and

3.11.2   The author's instinct is to delete the word 'contemplate' in two places because it is almost impossible to know with any degree of certainty what amounts to 'contemplation'. If 'contemplation' becomes reality then the landlord will actually set these grounds out in any notice he serves. The word is too vague and both uncertain and unfair.

3.11.4   The comments relating to the deletion of the word 'contemplation' in **clause 3.11.2** are equally applicable. The introduction of the word 'direct' should also assist the tenant by reinforcing this point. The amendment at the end of the clause is designed to ensure that the tenant's liability for costs in respect of any such claim is limited to a reasonable time after the end of the lease term and only in relation to wants of repair that have actually occurred during the contractual term. There can be few things more uncertain for a tenant than not knowing whether or not a schedule of dilapidation is coming. The longer the time lapse between the end of the term (or the date when the tenant vacates) and the date when the schedule is prepared and served on the tenant the more and more difficult it is to prove (from a landlord's point of view) that the disrepair is a result of the tenant's failure to comply with its repairing obligations rather than simply wear and tear by the passage of time. By imposing a contractual timescale, there is, at least, a cut-off point without having to rely on the statutory limitation periods in relation to the costs liability.

3.12.1   Landlords' advisers often prepare an initial draft lease which is often very heavily biased in favour of landlords. The need for indemnities anywhere in the lease should therefore be questioned by the tenant. As well as having all the tortious, contractual and self-help remedies

their use, and must indemnify the Landlord, and keep him indemnified, both during and following the end of the Term, against all losses in respect of any contravention of those Acts

3.12.2   Consent for applications

The Tenant must not make any application for planning permission without the consent of the Landlord such consent not to be unreasonably withheld or delayed PROVIDED ALWAYS that no such consent shall be required in relation to any applications made by the Tenant in relation to use of its usual corporate logo, signage or any items referred to in sub-clause 3.6.1 MASTS AND WIRES

3.12.3   Permissions and notices

The Tenant must obtain any planning permissions and serve any notices that may be required to carry out any development on or at the Premises

3.12.4   Charges and levies

Subject only to any statutory direction to the contrary, the Tenant must pay and satisfy any charge or levy that may subsequently be imposed under the Planning Acts in respect of carrying out or maintaining any development on or at the Premises

3.12.5   Preconditions for development

Notwithstanding any consent that may be granted by the Landlord under this Lease, the Tenant must not carry out any development on or at the Premises until all necessary notices under the Planning Acts have been served and copies produced to the Landlord, all necessary permissions under the Planning Acts have been obtained and produced to the Landlord, and the Landlord (acting reasonably) has acknowledged that every necessary planning permission is acceptable to him (such acknowledgement not to be unreasonably withheld or delayed). The Landlord may refuse to acknowledge his acceptance of a planning permission on the grounds that any condition contained in it or anything omitted from it or the period referred to in it would in the reasonable opinion of the Surveyor be, or be likely to be, prejudicial to the Landlord or to his reversionary interest in the Premises, the Building or any of his adjoining property whether during or following the end of the Term

3.12.6   Completion of development

Where a condition of any planning permission granted for development begun before the end of the Term requires works to be carried out to the Premises by a date after the end of the

available to a landlord to then seek an indemnity is, in the author's view, unfair to the tenant. Hence *all* references to indemnities from tenant to landlord in the lease have been deleted. It is, quite clearly, a question of the relative bargaining positions of the parties as to whether or not this is likely to be acceptable. The tenant should argue long and hard to ensure that his arguments win the day (see also note to **clause 3.14**).

3.12.2   The amendment prevents the tenant being held to ransom by the landlord and avoids a situation arising when the landlord is obliged to consent to an alteration or improvement but then does not give consent to the necessary planning application. The final amendment ensures the landlord cannot attempt to frustrate the tenant's legitimate commercial aspirations regarding use of its usual corporate identity.

3.12.5   While likely to be a very emotive issue for the landlord (on the grounds that any *development* which takes place may raise the possibility of a diminution in the value of his interest in the premises) the amendments are intended to ensure that in all the circumstances the landlord acts reasonably. An absolute prohibition with the consequent ability of a landlord to frustrate fair and reasonable requests from the tenant is likely, in reality, only to lead to one of two things: either an abuse of the landlord's dominant position or some form of ransom payment being required.

Term, the Tenant must, unless the Landlord directs otherwise, finish those works before the end of the Term

3.12.7   Security for compliance with conditions

In any case where a planning permission is granted subject to conditions, and if the Landlord reasonably so requires, the Tenant must provide sufficient security for his compliance with the conditions and must not implement the planning per-mission until the security has been provided

3.12.8   Appeal against refusal or conditions

If reasonably required by the Landlord to do so, but and at his own the Landlord's cost, the Tenant must appeal against any refusal of planning permission or the imposition of any condi-tions on a planning permission relating to the Premises fol-lowing an application for planning permission by the Tenant.

3.13   *Plans, documents and information*

3.13.1   Evidence of compliance with this Lease

If so requested (but not more than once in any calendar year), the Tenant must produce to the Landlord or the Surveyor any plans, documents and other evidence the Landlord reasonably requires to satisfy himself that the provisions of this Lease have been complied with

3.13.2   Information for renewal or rent review

3.13.2.1 If so requested, the Tenant must produce to the Landlord, the Surveyor or any person acting as the third party determining the Rent in default of agreement between the Landlord and the Tenant under the provisions for rent review contained in this Lease, any information requested in writing in relation to any pending or intended step under the 1954 Act or the imple-mentation of any provisions for rent review

3.13.2.1 if so requested, the Tenant must, within one month of the change taking place, notify the Landlord of any changes in his VAT status

3.14   Indemnities

The Tenant must keep the Landlord fully indemnified against all losses arising directly or indirectly out of any act, omission or negligence of the Tenant, or any persons at the Premises expressly or impliedly with his authority or any breach or non-observance by the Tenant of the covenants, conditions or other provisions of this Lease or any of the matters to which this demise is subject

3.12.7   The same points apply here as those stated above in relation to **clauses 3.12.2** and **3.12.5**.

3.12.8   If the failure to obtain planning consent following a tenant's application is likely to be detrimental to the landlord's interest, he may request that the tenant appeals against any planning refusal. If this is a decision made by the landlord then there is absolutely no reason why the landlord should not pay for it. If such an appeal is not likely to affect the tenant's ability to continue to use the premises for its permitted use (so that the tenant does not wish to appeal) then it would seem unreasonable for the landlord to request that such an appeal be made. The amendments seek to cater for both these concerns.

3.13.1   The author's natural inclination would be to delete this clause in its entirety. A landlord will have reserved powers to himself (eg rights of access to inspect) to satisfy himself that the tenant is complying with his obligation. This clause, unfairly, puts the onus on the tenant to prove that he is not in breach! The proposed amendments ensure that the landlord does not use this clause for nuisance value.

3.13.2.1 If landlord and tenant have been unable to agree the new level of rent, despite having tried to do so, then the provision is wholly unacceptable. Rent review negotiations and lease renewal negotiations are likely to be two occasions when there may be potential litigation between the parties. The tenant should not accept a provision whereby it is obliged to show its hand before being advised to do so by its professional advisers and clauses such as this should be strongly resisted if only for this reason. The compromise would be to give the information only 'if reasonably required'.

3.14   As was previously alluded to under **clause 3.12.1** in consequence of all the tortious, contractual, self-help and other remedies available to a landlord, a general indemnity is far too wide ranging to be readily acceptable to a tenant. Common law and statute adequately deals with the losses an aggrieved party can recover and an indemnity such as this goes beyond the general remoteness of damage test. It is the author's view that, as a matter of policy, indemnities should be resisted but, clearly, the outcome of this particular debate is going to be decided ultimately by the relative bargaining strengths

3.14   *Reletting boards and viewing*

Where the Tenant has no right or no longer has the right to a new lease of the Premises pursuant to the relevant provisions of the 1954 Act Tthe Tenant must permit the Landlord to enter the Premises at any reasonable time (on reasonable prior written notice) during the last 6 months of the Contractual Term and at any time thereafter and whenever the Lease Rents or any part of them are in arrear and unpaid (and not disputed) for longer than 14 21 days and to fix and retain anywhere on the Premises a board advertising them for reletting PROVIDED ALWAYS that any such notice shall make it clear that the business carried on by the Tenant at the Premises is unaffected. While any such board is on the Premises to which the Tenant has not objected the Tenant must permit viewing of them at reasonable times of the day on reasonable prior written notice

3.15   *Obstruction and encroachment*

3.15.1   **Obstruction of windows**

The Tenant must not knowingly stop up, darken or obstruct any window or light belonging to the Premises

3.15.2   **Encroachments**

The Tenant must at the Landlord's sole cost and expense take all reasonable steps to prevent the construction of any new window, light, opening, doorway, path, passage, pipe or the making of any encroachment or the acquisition of any easement in relation to the Premises and must notify the Landlord as soon as reasonably practicable after becoming aware of the same immediately if any such thing is constructed, encroachment is made or easement acquired, or if any attempt is made to encroach or acquire an easement. At the reasonable request and cost of the Landlord the Tenant must adopt such reasonable means as are required to prevent the making of any encroachment or the acquisition of any easement PROVIDED ALWAYS that the Tenant shall not be obliged by virtue of this subclause or any other provision contained in this Lease be obliged to take any steps likely to interfere with its beneficial use and occupation of the Premises in accordance with the provisions of the Lease

3.16   *Yielding up*

At the end of the Term the Tenant must yield up the Premises with vacant possession, decorated and repaired in accordance with and in the condition required by the provisions of this Lease, give up all keys of the Premises to the Landlord, remove tenant's fixtures and fittings if reasonably requested to do so by the Landlord (in writing) and remove all signs erect-

of the parties. Institutional landlords certainly have their own views! Tenants and their advisers must nevertheless appreciate fully the consequences of agreeing to such a clause. One possible compromise as a last resort is to limit the indemnity to losses arising from a breach of covenant by the tenant.

3.14 (new) If the tenant is likely to want to remain in the premises at the end of the term then, clearly, there is no need for the landlord to be looking to relet and many of the proposed amendments are likely to be unnecessary. However, it would be rare for a tenant to know its future intentions when the lease is being negotiated! Where, however, a tenant does not wish to remain in occupation the amendments seek to ensure that any viewing etc is undertaken so as to cause minimum disruption to the tenant's occupation.

3.15.1 The amendment here introduces the element of knowledge on the part of the tenant.

3.15.2 The matters with which this clause purports to deal with are ones which the landlord may, reasonably or otherwise, consider adversely affect the value of his reversionary interest. The amendments will prevent the tenant being out of pocket in seeking to maintain the status quo (and value!) of the landlord's reversion and ensure that any such works which are required are undertaken at the cost of the landlord and that they do not interfere with the tenant's occupation or use of the property.

3.16 It is absolutely fair that the landlord should have the property back at the end of the term decorated and repaired in accordance with the tenant's obligations set out in the lease. What is potentially contentious is whether or not fixtures and fittings which the tenant may be prepared to leave (and which may actually enhance the value or marketability of the premises) should be removed by the tenant, if indeed their ownership has not already passed to the landlord. If the fixtures should have been removed, then the tenant may well be in

ed by the Tenant or any of his predecessors in title in, on or near the Premises, ~~immediately~~ making good as soon as reasonably practicable any physical damage caused to the Premises by their removal

3.17 *Interest on arrears*

The Tenant must pay interest at the Default Interest Rate on any of the Lease Rents or other sums due under this Lease that are not paid within [21] days of ~~on~~ the date due, whether formally demanded or not~~, the interest to be recoverable as rent. Nothing in this clause is to entitle the Tenant to withhold or delay any payment of the Rent or any other sum due under this Lease or affect the rights of the Landlord in relation to any non-payment~~

3.18 *Statutory notices*

The Tenant must give the Landlord full particulars of any notice, direction, order or proposal relating to the Premises made, given or issued to the Tenant by any government department or local, public, regulatory or other authority or court as soon as reasonably practicable following ~~within 2 days of~~ receipt, and if so reasonably requested by the Landlord must produce it to the Landlord. The Tenant must as soon as reasonably practicable ~~without delay~~ take all ~~necessary~~ reasonable steps to comply with the notice, direction or order. At the request and cost of the Landlord, ~~but at his own cost,~~ the Tenant must make or join with the Landlord in making any objection or representation the Landlord deems expedient against or in respect of a notice, direction, order or proposal PROVIDED ALWAYS the Tenant shall not by virtue of the provisions of this clause or any other provision contained in this Lease be obliged to take or join in any such steps likely to affect its beneficial enjoyment or use of the Premises in

breach of an obligation to yield up the premises with vacant possession. The case of *Cumberland Consolidated Holdings Limited v Ireland* [1946] 1 KB 264 and the recent case of *John Laing Construction Limited v Amber Pass Limited* [2004] 17 EG 128 illustrate the pitfalls for a tenant. It is possible that a failure to remove not only fixtures but chattels and return the keys may lead to a dispute and litigation as to whether vacant possession has been yielded up. In the absence of agreement and for a fixed term tenancy the tenant's fixtures and fittings must be removed by the termination date of the lease. If not, the right to remove them is given up when possession is handed back to the landlord. The amendments seek to introduce the concept of reasonableness into this particular debate (and not leave it to be decided by the landlord from his own totally subjective viewpoint). The deletion of the reference to 'vacant possession' is important if the tenant is allowed under the lease to grant protected subleases since if this happens the tenant may not be able to comply with his obligation in this respect. The amendments towards the end of the clause seek to ensure that any liability in consequence of such removal by the tenant is limited to physical damage caused to the premises and does not extend to any form of pecuniary loss a landlord may claim.

3.17   Periods of grace are now fairly commonplace in commercial leases and this clause seeks to enshrine, contractually, a period of grace when payment of rent and other sums fall due. The tenant should not accept that interest be deemed recoverable as rent as this will enable the landlord to distrain and forfeit in the event of non-payment without the need for service of a s 146 Notice. Whilst the Common Law Procedure Act 1852 offers some comfort to the tenant this is best not left to chance. If a period of grace is accepted then, clearly, the second sentence in this clause can be deleted. Even if a period of grace is not acceptable to a landlord, a tenant should still seek to delete the second sentence to ensure that the clause does not conflict with any lease provisions dealing with set-off (see **clause 2.1.1**).

3.18   The amendments to the first two sentences will seek to ensure that there is no breach in failing to notify the landlord within the time period stated. There may be a multitude of reasons why it is not possible to comply with the strict timetable set out and the amendment caters for these eventualities. The amendment dealing with the cost of compliance ensures that, particularly in relation to short-term lettings, the tenant is not out of pocket. The fairness of such a provision would have to be judged in the overall context of the transaction. The proviso seeks to ensure that the tenant is not obliged to take any steps likely to affect its occupation and use of the property.

accordance with the provisions of this Lease and PROVIDED
FURTHER that the Tenant need not comply with any such
notice or order whilst an appeal is being properly pursued
against such notice or order

3.19 *Keyholders*

The Tenant must ensure that at all times the Landlord has [and
the local police force have] written notice of the name, home
address and home telephone number of one at least 2 key-
holders of the Premises

3.20 *Viewing on sale of reversion*

The Tenant must at any reasonable time during the Term and
on reasonable prior written notice, permit prospective purchasers of the Landlord's reversion or any other interest superior to the Term, or agents instructed in connection with the
sale of the reversion or such an interest, to view the Premises
without interruption provided they have the prior written
authority of the Landlord or his agents

3.21 *Defective premises*

As soon as reasonably practicable after becoming aware of
the same Tthe Tenant must give notice to the Landlord of any
defect in the Premises that might give rise to an obligation on
the Landlord to do or refrain from doing anything in order to
comply with the provisions of this Lease or the duty of care
imposed on the Landlord, whether pursuant to the Defective
Premises Act 1972 or otherwise, and must at all times display
and maintain any reasonable notices the Landlord from time
to time reasonably requires him to display at the Premises

3.22 *Replacement guarantor*

3.22.1 Guarantor replacement events

In this clause 3.23 references to a 'guarantor replacement
event' are references, in the case of an individual, to death,
bankruptcy, having a receiving order made against him or
having a receiver appointed under the Mental Health Act 1983,
and, in the case of a company, to passing a resolution to wind
up, entering into liquidation or having a receiver appointed

3.22.2 Action on occurrence of a guarantor replacement event

Where during the relevant Liability Period a guarantor replacement event occurs to the Guarantor or any person who has
entered into an authorised guarantee agreement, the Tenant
must as soon as reasonably practicable after becoming aware
of the same give notice of the event to the Landlord within 14

3.19   There may be circumstances where it is totally inappropriate to have this clause in a lease of office premises in any event whether the police need to be involved will vary from letting to letting. However, it is likely to be in the tenant's interest as much as the landlord that this information is available, eg in the case of burglary. It may be however that, depending on the circumstances of the particular letting, it is not possible to give details of *two* key holders and one may have to suffice.

3.20   The amendments to this clause give the tenant an element of control over when people view the premises with the potential for disruption and rumours this may cause (see **clause 3.8.1**).

3.21   It is unlikely that as soon as a defect manifests itself in the premises the tenant will be aware of it (unless there is something patently obvious) and even more unlikely that the tenant (or at least the employees within the premises) will be aware that the existence of such a defect imposes a statutory duty on the landlord! The amendments to this clause aim to deal with these concerns from a tenant's point of view and strike a fair balance between the obligations on the part of the tenant and the statutory duties on the part of the landlord.

3.22.2 Ideally this clause should be ditched in its entirety. It may be extremely difficult for a tenant to find a substitute guarantor. In the event that it is possible it is vital to ensure a formal release is obtained for the original guarantor. The first amendment to this clause is self-explanatory. Bearing in mind the nature of *guarantor replacement events* it will not always be possible for the tenant to be aware of such matters. A short fixed timetable is therefore unaccept-

~~days of his becoming aware of it.~~ If so reasonably required by the Landlord, the Tenant must within 28 days use all reasonable endeavours to obtain some other person or corporate body reasonably acceptable to the Landlord to execute a guarantee in the form of the Guarantor's covenants in clause 6 GUARANTEE PROVISIONS or the authorised guarantee agreement in Schedule 8 THE AUTHORISED GUARANTEE AGREEMENT, as the case may be, for the residue of the relevant Liability Period and upon the execution of such an alternative guarantee the original guarantor or person who has entered into the authorised guarantee agreement and/or their estates shall be unconditionally released from all past present or future liability

3.23   *Exercise of the Landlord's rights*

Subject to the provisions of clause 4.4 ~~T~~the Tenant must permit the Landlord to exercise any of the rights granted to him by virtue of the provisions of this Lease at all times during the Term without interruption or interference

3.24   *The Office Covenants*

The Tenant must observe and perform the Office Covenants

3.25   *The Services*

The Tenant must observe and perform his obligations contained in Schedule 6 THE SERVICE CHARGE AND SERVICES

3.26   *Registration*

3.26.1   Obligation to register

If this Lease or the rights granted or reserved by this Lease are registered or registrable at HM Land Registry then the Tenant must:

(a)   register this Lease and any assignment or other registrable disposition of this Lease at HM Land Registry within ([   ]) of the date of this Lease or the date of the instrument of assignment or other disposition requiring registration as the case may be

(b)   use his ~~best~~ reasonable endeavours to procure that all rights granted or reserved by this Lease are properly noted against the titles that are affected by them and

(c)   within (state period eg 7 days) of the registration of the grant assignment or other registrable ([   ]) disposition of this Lease or the registration of notice

able. The next three amendments are also self-explanatory and introduce the concepts of a replacement guarantor being 'reasonably required', the tenant using 'all reasonable endeavours' and the replacement guarantor being 'reasonably acceptable' to the landlord. These amendments meet the situation where the status of the tenant has changed during the time the guarantee has subsisted so that it would, by an objective standard, no longer be reasonable to request a guarantor. The final amendment ensures, for the avoidance of doubt, that there is no duplication from the tenant's point of view and no dispute as to whether or not the original guarantor or any party who has entered into the authorised guarantee agreement is still potentially liable as the amendment expressly provides for his release.

3.23   The amendment provides that any access rights exercised by the landlord are exercised in accordance with a landlord's covenant contained in new **clause 4.4**.

3.26   The amendment is self-explanatory, although it should be noted that in the light of *IBM United Kingdom Ltd v Rockware Glass Ltd* (1980) FSR, 335 CA it may be that there is little practical difference between a covenant to use best endeavours and a covenant to use reasonable endeavours.

against the titles affected by the rights granted or reserved by this Lease as the case may be deliver to the Landlord official copies of the registered title or titles

3.26.2   Failure to register

The Landlord shall not be liable to the Tenant for the Tenant's failure to register or protect this Lease or any rights granted by this Lease

3.26   *Costs of grant of this lease*

The Tenant must pay the fees and disbursements of the Landlord's solicitors, agents and surveyors and all other costs and expenses incurred by the Landlord in relation to the negotiation, preparation, execution and grant of this lease and the stamp duty on the counterpart

3.27   *Consent to the Landlord's release*

The Tenant must not unreasonably withhold consent to a request made by the Landlord under the 1995 Act section 8 for a release from all or any of the landlord covenants of this Lease

3.27   It is to be hoped in today's climate that the old practice of tenants having to be responsible for landlord's costs has now, to a large extent, fallen by the wayside. Tenants have their own legal fees to pay and there can be, in the author's view, no sustainable reason why on the grant of a lease the tenant should pick up both his own legal (and other) costs and those of the landlord. Indeed the Costs of Leases Act 1958 states that each party should pay their own costs (in the absence of agreement).

Landlords will often argue that it is a historical convention but during recessionary times the author certainly has acted on a number of occasions for tenants when landlords actually agreed to pay the tenant's fees! Should tenants therefore be arguing for a shifting convention? As the property market follows its normal cyclical path of undersupply/overdemand and vice versa with the consequential shift in the relative bargaining strengths of landlords and tenants, tenants can in the appropriate marketplace insist that each party is responsible for its own costs! One interesting point to bear in mind in relation to this particular issue is that just because the original lease contained a provision obliging the tenant to pay the landlord's legal costs for the grant of the lease then this provision will *not* always be included in a renewed lease (*Cairnplace Ltd v CBL (Property Investment) Co Ltd* [1984] 1 All ER 315, CA). If the tenant has agreed in negotiations to pay the landlord's legal costs, it would be sensible for the tenant to seek agreement for these costs being capped by agreeing to pay a fixed sum for the landlord's legal costs or an agreed sum as 'a contribution' towards these.

The notes to **Recommendation 3 of the Code** broadly correspond with the notes above, ie costs are a matter for negotiation between the parties but reference is made to the 1958 Costs of Leases Act..

3.28   This appears at first sight a useful (and clever) clause from a land-

4   THE LANDLORD'S COVENANTS

The Landlord covenants with the Tenant to observe and perform the requirements of this clause 4

4.1   *Quiet enjoyment*

The Landlord covenants with the Tenant to permit the Tenant peaceably and quietly to hold and enjoy the Premises without any interruption or disturbance from or by the Landlord or any person claiming under or in trust for him or by title paramount

4.2   *The Services*

4.2.1   Provision of the Services

~~If the Tenant pays the service charge and observes his obligations under this Lease,~~ Tthe Landlord must use his best ~~reasonable~~ endeavours to provide the Services

lord's point of view if he can get away with it! In *Avonridge Property Co Limited v Mashru* [2005] 01 EG 100 the House of Lords held that the parties to a lease entered into after 1 January 1996 (a new lease) were entitled to limit their liability in whatever way they might agree. Section 25 of the Landlord and Tenant (Covenants) Act 1995 was designed to prevent the liability of a party being extended and did not operate to prevent that liability being limited. Tenants should be reluctant to agree to the limitation on the landlord's liability in this way where the landlord is giving significant covenants, eg repair or the provision of services. A landlord should be content in the knowledge that if a tenant unreasonably objects to the landlord being released when he sells the reversion he does have a statutory right to apply to the courts for a release.

4　THE LANDLORD'S COVENANTS

4.1　This amendment, while often missed by tenants and not readily accepted by landlords, is really quite vital from a tenant's point of view. Without reference to *title paramount*, the landlord is only liable for the acts of persons in so far as they are his successors in title or have authority from him to do the acts of which the tenant is complaining. So if a subtenant holds premises under a lease containing a limited quiet enjoyment covenant on the part of his landlord (eg a clause where there is no reference to title paramount) only for the subtenant to be evicted by the head landlord because the head rent has not been paid, this does *not* constitute a breach of the covenant for quiet enjoyment by the tenant's landlord and no claim for damages can be made against him. The words must be included. As to the interaction of the landlord's covenant for quiet enjoyment and his covenant to repair, see *Speiro Lechouritis v Goldmile Properties Limited* [2003] 125 EG 143 where the Court held that the two covenants were to be reconciled by requiring the landlord to use 'all reasonable precautions' (rather than all possible precautions) to minimise disturbance to the tenant when carrying out repairs.

4.2.1　The first part of the amendment deletes the precondition requirement for provision of the services. In reality it will be virtually impossible for a landlord to police and operate such a precondition, especially in the case of a multi-let building. If one tenant defaults on a precondition is the landlord going to cut off provision of the services to all the occupiers? This is obviously most unlikely and, therefore, the precondition is in many instances a nonsense and does not provide any realistic sanction against the tenant. An additional reason for its deletion would be to ensure that if a tenant, for example, was in arrears on the service charge payments (eg because of a dispute) he would still be able to bring an action against the landlord for non-performance of the services and would not be barred out. The second amendment seeks to impose on the landlord the highest possible duty to provide what will no doubt be vitally important services required by the tenant (see **clause 5.6.3.1**).

4.2.2   Relief from liability

The Landlord is not to be liable to the Tenant for any breach of his obligations under clause 4.2.1, where the breach is caused by something beyond his control (provided he uses reasonable endeavours to remedy the breach) except to the extent that the breach:

4.2.2.1   could have been prevented or

4.2.2.2   its consequences could have been lessened or

4.2.2.3   the time during which its consequences were experienced could have been shortened by the exercise of reasonable skill by the Landlord or those undertaking the obligation on his behalf

4.2.3   Variation and withholding of the Services

The Landlord may add to, withhold or vary the Services if (acting reasonably) he considers the addition, withholding or variation will improve the amenities in the Building for the benefit of the Tenant and the other tenants in the Building or enable the management of the Building to be more efficiently conducted even if it increases the Landlord's Expenses (provided the Tenant's beneficial use and enjoyment of the Premises is not impaired or interfered with) or if he is required to do so by a competent authority

4.2.4   Special services

Any services rendered to the Tenant by staff employed by the Landlord, other than services referred to in paragraph 3 of Schedule 6, are to be deemed to be special services for which, and for the consequences of which, the Tenant will be entirely responsible. The Tenant is not to be entitled to any services from such staff that may in any way whatever interfere with the performance of their duties to the Landlord

4.3   *Similar Leases*

The Landlord covenants with the Tenant not to allow any other party to occupy all or any parts of the Building other than pursuant to a lease in materially the same form as this Lease including (for the avoidance of doubt) the provisions of Schedule 6

4.4   *Exercising Rights*

In exercising the rights reserved to the Landlord by this Lease which involve entry on to the Premises the Landlord must:

4.2.2   Ideally the tenant would wish to delete this clause in its entirety and argue that an exclusion clause would need to comply with the provisions of section 2 of the Unfair Contract Terms Act 1977. However, the question of whether or not that particular piece of legislation applies to service charge provisions contained in a lease is unresolved and has been the subject of much academic debate. If the exclusion clause is caught by the Unfair Contract Terms Act 1977 then the qualified covenant approach adopted here, which seeks to limit the circumstances in which the landlord will be in breach, may indeed satisfy the requirements of section 2 of the Act.

4.2.3   The first amendment to this clause brings an element of objectivity to determining what additional services may be in the interests of the tenant (and other tenants in the same building). The second amendment seeks to reinforce this. The proviso prohibits any variation or change to the services which would or might result in the tenant being left in a situation which is detrimental to his occupation and use.

4.3
(new)   This additional covenant imposes on the landlord an obligation to grant leases to other tenants in the building on terms materially the same to ensure that there is an element of management consistency and this, coupled with the provisions contained in **clause 4.5 (new)** below, gives the tenant the comfort of knowing that other parties occupy the building on broadly similar terms and will, for example, be making service charge payments. Hence the specific mention of Schedule 6 which deals with service charges. This will help reassure the tenant that nothing is likely to occur in other parts of the building which is likely to be detrimental to his own occupation, although, if the detriment to the tenant was serious, this might well amount to a breach of the landlord's obligation not to derogate from his grant. See *Chartered Trust plc v Davies* [1997] 2 EGLR 83 and *K – Sultana Saeed v Plustrade* [2002] EWCA Civ 2011. The danger to the landlord is that this could create a letting scheme, which would enable a tenant to directly enforce a user covenant in a neighbour's lease without the landlord's assistance. See *Williams v Kiley* [2002] EWCA Civ 1645. It may therefore be sensible for the landlord to expressly negative in the lease the application of this doctrine as well as the Contracts (Rights of Third Parties Act) 1999. See the amendment to clause 8.18 of the Lease.

4.4
(new)   This clause is self-explanatory. Landlords may well baulk at such a provision, but the author's view is that it is perfectly fair and reasonable although for the reasons given at **clause 3.14** (deleted) the landlord could legitimately resist the indemnity referred to in **clause 4.4.3**.

4.4.1   cause and ensure that those exercising such rights on its behalf cause as little damage as is possible to the Premises and as little disturbance and inconvenience as possible to the Tenant and occupier of the Premises

4.4.2   make good (at its own sole cost and expense) any damage caused in the exercise of such right and

4.4.3   indemnify the Tenant and any other occupiers of the Premises and keep them indemnified against all damage and loss suffered by them arising directly or indirectly out of the exercise of such right

4.5   *Enforcing Covenants*

The Landlord covenants to enforce the covenants on the part of the tenants contained in other leases in the Building

4.6   *Environmental Matters*

The Landlord covenants that it will as soon as reasonably practicable and at its own sole cost and expense undertake any works in relation to the Building required to comply with any environmental regulation, condition or legislation PROVIDED ALWAYS that no such cost or expense should be recharged to the tenants in the Building via the service charge or otherwise

4.7   *Inherent Defects*

The Landlord shall at its own expense, remedy any Inherent Defect of whose existence the Tenant shall, during the Term, have notified the Landlord and any want of repair which is attributable to any such Inherent Defect and which manifests itself at any time during the Term

4.5
(new)

This new clause, coupled with **clause 4.3 (new)** above, protects the position of the tenant by ensuring that nothing untoward is done by any other tenant in the building which is likely to detrimentally affect the complaining tenant's own use and occupation. The traditional view was that the covenant for quiet enjoyment granted by the landlord was *not* sufficient either to enable one tenant to bring an action against his landlord for his failure to ensure that another tenant complied with his contractual obligations contained in his own lease or to bring an action directly against the defaulting tenant. Tenants may now be able to rely on the recent decision in *Chartered Trust plc v Davies* [1997] 2 EGLR 83, CA, where it was held that there was a duty on the landlord in certain circumstances to ensure that one tenant's use of premises did not materially interfere with the use and enjoyment of other premises by a neighbouring tenant. However, it is much better to try and deal with the matter specifically and this clause attempts to do this. A compromise, if a landlord resists is to agree to inclusion of the clause, '... *at the cost of the tenant ...*'.

4.6

The landlord will either have satisfied himself about the environmental status of the site or the building prior to its construction (a site survey, warranties from an environmental consultant, etc) or make due enquiries of a vendor to ensure it has adequate protection. A landlord who baulks at a clause like this should be put to proof as to what he knows about the site which causes him to reject the principle. This clause barely scratches the surface of an issue like this. A much more comprehensive precedent dealing with the principles highlighted in this clause can be found in *Ross: Commercial Leases* – Precedent 30.

4.7

As it has already been explained, unless the tenant has adequate protection elsewhere in relation to inherent defects which manifest themselves in the Premises or the Building of which they form part, it should not accept these matters as being within the ambit of its repairing obligation (see note to **clause 3.4.1**). This new clause seeks to impose the obligation to make good any such matters on the landlord. It is difficult to envisage circumstances where the landlord may argue against such a provision, especially in relation to a new build where the landlord has failed to mitigate the hardship

4.8   *Headlease*

4.8.1   The Landlord covenants to pay the rent[s] reserved by the Headlease, and to perform (so far as the Tenant is not liable for such performance under the terms of this Lease) the covenants and conditions on the part of the lessee contained in the Headlease and to indemnify and to keep indemnified the Tenant against all actions claims proceedings costs expenses and demands in any way relating to the Headlease, and if the Tenant shall at any time pay any sum or sums or money or sustain or incur any loss damage or expense for or on account of the rent[s] reserved by the Headlease or as a result of a breach of the covenants and conditions on the part of the lessee contained in the Headlease where the Tenant is not liable for such performance under the terms of this Lease, then the Tenant may retain the Lease Rents reserved by this Lease until there shall, by such retention or otherwise be fully paid and satisfied all and every sum or sums of money loss damage or expense as mentioned above

4.8.2   the Landlord covenants with the Tenant not to agree to any variation of the terms of the Headlease without further obtaining the Tenant"s consent

4.8.4   the Landlord covenants to use its best endeavours to enforce the covenants on the part of the lessor contained in the Headlease

4.8.5   the Landlord covenants to use its best endeavours to obtain the consent of the lessor to the Headlease whenever the Tenant makes application for any consent required under this Lease where the consent of both the Landlord and the lessor to the Headlease is required pursuant to the terms of this Lease

potentially caused to the tenant by ensuring that the professionals engaged in the design and construction have given collateral warranties or duty of care agreements in favour of the tenant. If the landlord continues to refuse any such provision, and the tenant is in a situation where, potentially at least, it could be liable to make good any such inherent defects, the tenant must consider ensuring there is a provision in the Lease, whereby the landlord will reimburse the tenant for any costs and expenses it incurs in making good any such inherent defects and ensuring that there is excluding from any service charge liability, the cost of having to make good any such matters.

4.8   The additional clauses added in here are included to protect the tenant in a sub-lease situation. All are self-explanatory.

5   INSURANCE

5.1   *Warranty as to convictions*

The Tenant warrants that before the execution of this document he has disclosed to the Landlord in writing any conviction, judgment or finding of any court or tribunal of which it is aware relating to the Tenant or any director, other officer or major shareholder of the Tenant of such a nature as to be likely to affect the decision of any insurer or underwriter to grant or to continue insurance of any of the Insured Risks

5.2   *Covenant to insure*

The Landlord covenants with the Tenant to insure the Building,[in the joint names of the Landlord and the Tenant] if the Tenant pays the Insurance Rent, unless the insurance is vitiated by any act of the Tenant or by anyone at the Building expressly or by implication with his authority and under his control

5.3   *Details of the insurance*

5.3.1   Office, underwriters and agency

Insurance is to be effected in such reputable and substantial insurance office in the UK or whose principal office is in the UK, or with such underwriters, and through such reputable and substantial agency as the Landlord (acting reasonably) from time to time decides

5.3.2   Insurance cover

Insurance must be effected for the following amounts:

5   **INSURANCE**

> **Recommendation 8 of the Code: Insurance:** *Where the landlord is responsible for insuring the property, the policy terms should be competitive. The tenant of an entire building should, in appropriate cases, be given the opportunity to influence the choice of insurer. If the premises are so damaged by an uninsured risk as to prevent occupation, the tenant should be allowed to terminate the lease unless the landlord agrees to rebuild at his own cost.*

> **Recommendation 14 of the Code: Insurance:** *Where the landlord has arranged insurance, the terms should be made known to the tenant and any interest of the tenant covered by the policy. Any material change in the insurance should be notified to the tenant. Tenants should consider taking out their own insurance against loss or damage to contents and their business (loss of profits etc.) and any other risks not covered by the landlord's policy.*

5.1   It may simply not be possible for a tenant to know all of the convictions, judgments, etc which may exist against all the people listed. If a company is a shareholder of the corporate tenant what steps must the tenant take to pierce the corporate veil? The amendment seeks to reflect this.

5.2   The first amendment is in square brackets because, in this scenario, it is extremely unlikely a landlord would accept it. It would not be practical for the landlord to insure a multi-tenanted building in various names. The best such a tenant is likely to get is a note of his interest being made on the policy (see new **clause 5.9.2**). As in **clause 4.2.1**, the original drafting here seeks to impose a precondition to the landlord's covenant to insure. The same arguments apply here as those stated above in relation to **clause 4.2.1**. The second amendment provides that the tenant is not responsible for any member of the general public who enters the premises as licensee, contractor, statutory undertaker, etc. The additional (and in the author's view essential) element of control seeks, at least, to restrict the category of persons who can vitiate the insurance and to make the clause more objective and better balanced.

5.3.1   This amendment is self-explanatory and seeks to ensure that as much as possible is done by the landlord to ensure that, should there ever be a need to claim under the insurance policy, the insurance company has not disappeared. By stipulating the UK it will be easier to trace what has happened, if anything untoward has indeed happened. The final element to the amendment seeks to ensure that once again there is an element of objectivity as to which insurance office, underwriters or agency the landlord chooses to insure through.

5.3.2.1   the <u>reasonable and proper</u> sum that the Landlord is from time
to time advised <u>by his Surveyor</u> is the full cost of rebuilding
and reinstating the Building <u>(at the time of such reinstatement)</u>, including ~~VAT~~ architects', surveyors', engineers', solicitors' and all other professional persons' fees, the fees payable
on any applications for planning permission or other permits
or consents that may be required in relation to rebuilding or
reinstating the Building, the <u>reasonable and proper</u> cost of
preparation of the site including shoring-up, debris removal,
demolition, site clearance and any works that may be required
by statute, and incidental expenses and

5.3.2.2   loss of rental and service charge income from the Building,
taking account of any rent review that may be due, for 3 years
or such longer period <u>(not exceeding 4 years)</u> as the Landlord
from time to time <u>reasonably</u> requires for planning and carrying out the rebuilding or reinstatement <u>PROVIDED ALWAYS
that the acceptance by the Tenant of any estimation of the
reviewed rent made by the Landlord pursuant to the provisions of this sub-clause for the purpose of establishing the
level of loss of rent cover shall not be deemed to be an acceptance by the Tenant that the actual rent following a Review Date
should equate to this level</u>

5.3.3   Risks insured

Insurance must be effected against damage or destruction by
any of the Insured Risks to the extent that such insurance may
ordinarily be arranged <u>with a substantial and reputable insur-
er</u> for properties such as the Building, subject to such excess-
es, exclusions or limitations as the insurer <u>reasonably</u> requires
<u>and are accepted as common practice in the insurance market</u>

5.4   *Payment of the Insurance Rent*

The Tenant covenants to pay the Insurance Rent for the period
starting on the commencement date of the Term and ending
on the day before the next policy renewal date on the date of
this document, and subsequently to pay the Insurance Rent on
demand ~~and, if so demanded, in advance of the policy renewal date~~

5.5   *Suspension of the Rent*

5.5.1   Events giving rise to suspension

If and whenever the Building or any part of it <u>or any access
way or ways (or any part of them) to it or any essential services to it</u> is <u>or are</u> damaged or destroyed by one or more of the
Insured Risks <u>or Uninsured Risks</u> except one against which
insurance may not ordinarily be arranged <u>with a substantial
and reputable insurer</u> for properties such as the Building

5.3.2.1　The first amendment to this clause seeks to ensure that the landlord does not over- or under-insure and, once again, brings the surveyor into play to exercise his professional judgement in a proper and ethical manner. The third addition avoids any timing confusion. Reference to VAT has been deleted on the basis that the additional expense of insuring against any VAT which may be payable on any reinstatement costs will not be justified if the landlord has opted to tax and is able to recover that VAT. The final amendment brings into play an objective element as regards costs.

5.3.2.2　This amendment is self-explanatory, bringing into play an element of reasonableness. The proviso at the end of the sub-clause is simply designed to ensure the tenant is not fixed with any form of agreement to an arbitrary level of rent which the landlord may have 'guestimated' for the purpose of its loss of rent insurance.

5.3.3　This amendment ties in the landlord's covenant with the obligation contained in **clause 5.3.1**.

5.4　The deletion at the end of this clause ensures that it is only once the policy premium demand is made by the insurance company that the tenant is obliged to reimburse. As has been stated earlier (see **clause 1.16**), the rationale behind insurance rent is simply that it is a *reimbursement* of monies laid out by the landlord.

5.5.1　The first amendment seeks to ensure that, if the premises remain undamaged but are inaccessible or unusable because of damage to access ways or corridors or other means of access or essential services then, even though in strict terms the premises are not damaged, since they cannot be used by the tenant the rent suspension provisions will, nevertheless, kick in. The other amendments to the clause narrow down the circumstances where the rent suspension will cease to operate so that the tenant could be required to commence

unless the Landlord has in fact insured against that risk so that the Premises are unfit for immediate occupation and ~~or~~ use by the Tenant , and ~~payment of the~~ save to the extent that insurance money is ~~not wholly or partly~~ refused by reason ~~because~~ of any act or default of the Tenant or anyone at the Building expressly or by implication with his authority and under his control then the provisions of clause 5.5.2 SUSPENDING THE RENT are to have effect

5.5.2   Suspending the Rent

In the circumstances mentioned in clause 5.5.1 EVENTS GIVING RISE TO SUSPENSION, the Lease Rents or a fair proportion of the Lease Rents according to the nature and the extent of the damage sustained, is to cease to be payable until a period of 3 months after the Building the Premises or access way or ways or essential services have ~~has~~ been rebuilt or reinstated so as to render the Premises fit for immediate occupation and use by the Tenant, or until the end of 3 years from the destruction or damage whichever period is the shorter, the proportion of the Lease Rents suspended and any dispute as to the proportion of the Rent suspended and the period of the suspension to be determined in accordance with the Arbitration Act 1996 by an arbitrator to be appointed by agreement between the Landlord and the Tenant or in default by the President or other proper officer for the time being of the Royal Institution of Chartered Surveyors upon the application of either the Landlord or the Tenant

rental payments again. The damage or destruction may not simply be as a result of an Insured Risk. The addition of the words 'or uninsured risks' (see definition in **clause 1.49**) ensure that damage as a result of terrorism (whether an insured risk or not) and other uninsured risks, for example: flooding, subsidence or landslip causes the suspension of rent payments. In our lease here we need to focus on the fact that a particular tenant is occupying particular premises and, therefore, those premises must be suitable for his immediate needs; hence the amendment to ensure that the premises must be made fit for immediate use and occupation by the specific tenant before that tenant becomes liable to pay rent again. A further period of rent suspension will compensate for any time required by the tenant to fit out the damaged premises. As originally drafted the clause makes the tenant liable for the entire consequences of insurance vitiation even if only part of the insurance monies have been refused and the penultimate amendment seeks to deal with that. The final amendment is restrictive once again in the tenant's favour so that the tenant is not responsible for the acts of anyone on the premises with authority but over whom the tenant has no control.

One other consideration which needs to be borne in mind by the tenant when settling this part of the lease relate to the possibility that, following its construction, it could be discovered that the building of which the premises forms part has been constructed on a contaminated site. It would be as well, at the outset, to incorporate a provision such that if the building, premises or any access ways to the premises are found to have been constructed on a contaminated site and until the clean-up operation is finalised, then once again the rent should be suspended. The same rights to terminate on the tenant's part should be included for such an eventuality. An excellent detailed provision excluding any liability on the part of the tenant for any such matters can be found in *Ross: Commercial Leases* (Precedent 30).

5.5.2   It should be noted that the definition of 'Lease Rents' in **clause 1.34** includes both the Service Charge and the Insurance Rent so that these also will be suspended. It is manifestly unfair for a tenant to have to pay any of these items if his premises are unusable. The reference to three months is simply to take account of any period required for tenant fitting out. The balance of the amendments are included for the same reasons as referred to in **clause 5.5.1**. A final point to bear in mind in relation to this clause relates to the limitation period for which payment of rent by virtue of the insurance policy subsists. Ideally there should be no time limit expressed but if there is one it should tie in with the time period within which the tenant can terminate the lease and walk away (see **clause 5.6.4** as amended) because, theoretically at least, at the end of the stated three-year period the tenant could become contractually liable to pay the rent etc again. A tenant would not thank his advisers if all that was left was the nebulous and undecided '*frustration*' argument.

5.6   *Reinstatement and termination*

5.6.1   Obligation to obtain permissions

If and whenever the Building or any part of it~~is~~ or any access way or ways or any essential services to it are damaged or destroyed by one or more of the Insured Risks except one against which insurance may not ordinarily be arranged with a substantial and reputable insurer for properties such as the Building unless the Landlord has in fact insured against that risk, and payment of the insurance money is not wholly or partly refused because of any act or default of the Tenant or anyone at the Building expressly or by implication with his authority and under his control then the Landlord must use ~~reasonable~~ best endeavours to obtain any planning permissions or other permits and consents ('permissions') that are required under the Planning Acts or otherwise to enable him to rebuild and reinstate the Building or the access way or ways or any essential services PROVIDED ALWAYS the Landlord will ensure that any rebuilding and reinstatement works are carried out in a good and workmanlike manner with the best quality materials available and in accordance with current good building practice having due regard to the reasonable requirements of the Tenant and will procure from the professional term engaged in the design rebuilding or reinstatement, collateral warranties in relation to the design, rebuilding or reinstatement works they have undertaken in a form to be approved by the Tenant (such approval not to be unreasonably withheld or delayed)

5.6.2   Obligation to reinstate

Subject to the provisions of clause 5.6.3 RELIEF FROM THE OBLIGATION TO REINSTATE, and, if any permissions are required, after they have been obtained, the Landlord must as soon as reasonably practicable apply all money received in respect of such insurance (except sums in respect of loss of the Rent) making up any shortfall out of its own monies and also the lack of insurance monies as a result of the damage or destruction being caused by Terrorism in rebuilding or reinstating the parts of the Building the access way or ways or essential services destroyed or damaged

5.6.3   Relief from the obligation to reinstate

The Landlord need not rebuild or reinstate the Building if and for so long as the rebuilding or reinstating is prevented because:

5.6.1   The same rationale applies here in respect of the proposed amendments as that referred to in **clause 5.5.1** above. The additional
wording at the end of the clause seeks to put the tenant into a similar position to that of a tenant of a newly constructed or wholly
refurbished premises or building.

5.6.2   The first amendment ensures that if, for whatever reason, the landlord has not insured for the full reinstatement value, then the tenant
is not penalised. Without this amendment if there is a shortfall then
the premises may end up only partially reinstated. The case of
Adami v Lincoln Garage Management Ltd ([1998] 17 EG 148, CA)
states that there is no implied obligation to spend anything more
than the insurance money it receives under the terms of the policy.
This amendment seeks to ensure that, if nothing else, at least the
landlord will take great care to ensure that he has sufficient insurance cover in place so that he doesn't have to fund any shortfall
himself. In any event the tenant will be funding the insurance premium via the insurance rent so it is difficult to see any sort of sustainable argument on the part of the landlord as to why this
amendment should not be included and the tenant should hold out
for this amendment.

5.6.3.1 the Landlord, despite using ~~reasonable~~ best endeavours, can- |
not obtain a necessary permission

5.6.3.2 any permission is granted subject to a lawful condition with
which in all the circumstances it is unreasonable to expect the
Landlord to comply because the cost in so doing would be out
of all proportion to the cost of otherwise rebuilding or reinstating

5.6.3.3 there is some defect or deficiency in the site on which the
rebuilding or reinstatement is to take place that means it can
only be undertaken at a cost that is unreasonable in all the circumstances

5.6.3.4 the Landlord is unable to obtain access to the site to rebuild or
reinstate

5.6.3.5 the rebuilding or reinstating is prevented by war, act of God,
government action, ~~strike or lock-out~~ or |

because of the occurrence of any other circumstances beyond
the Landlord's reasonable control

5.6.4 Notice to terminate

If the Premises are still not fit for the Tenant's immediate occupation and use or the access way or ways or essential services have not been reinstated so that at the end of a period of ~~3~~
2 years and 9 months starting on the date of the damage or
destruction, ~~the Landlord~~ either party may by notice served on
the ~~Tenant~~ other at any time ~~within 6 months of~~ after the end
of that period ('a notice to terminate following failure to reinstate') implement the provisions of clause 5.6.5 TERMINATION
FOLLOWING FAILURE TO REINSTATE

5.6.3.1 Certain cases have suggested that there is little practical difference between a covenant to use 'best endeavours', a covenant to use 'reasonable endeavours' and a covenant to 'take all reasonable steps'. However, the decision in *UBH (Mechanical Services) Ltd v Standard Life Assurance Co* (1986) Times, 13 November, indicates that the latter two forms of obligation may mean something less than 'best' endeavours. The author contends that this is one of the circumstances where there has to be an obligation on the landlord to use best (as opposed to anything else) endeavours because the tenant is threatened with losing his interest in the premises which, by reason of its location or otherwise, may be critical to his business.

5.6.3.2 The amendment at the end of this clause is self-explanatory and seeks to define and limit the circumstances in which the provisions would apply.

5.6.3.5 It is the author's view that strike or lockout can in many instances with appropriate steps on the landlord's part be prevented. These are political matters for the landlord to resolve and are, at least on most occasions of a short-term nature only and within the sphere of influence of the landlord. The other items listed are conceded as being outside his control!

5.6.4 The amendments here provide that it is not only the landlord who has the ability to terminate the lease if there is a delay in reinstating the premises' accessways or services such that the tenant cannot have back what was granted to him by the lease. It is the author's view that of the two parties the landlord is the one most likely to want to reinstate the premises, reinstate the tenant and ensure his investment retained its value. However, clearly, the tenant himself has business needs which will need to be satisfied and the tenant will not be in a position to wait around indefinitely while the landlord decides whether or not to obtain the relevant permissions and reinstate the premises. The time periods attempt to dovetail together to ensure that during the period of rent suspension there is no chance of the landlord calling upon the tenant to recommence rental payments. Ideally speaking, once the premises have been badly damaged or destroyed the tenant may want to have the ability to walk away and relocate almost immediately rather than wait for a considerable period while the premises are reinstated. If this is the case then a shorter period than that currently specified in **clause 5.6.4** should be negotiated. Total destruction of a building might be an event where the courts would apply the doctrine of frustration. In *National Carriers Limited v Panalpina (Northern) Limited* [1981] AC 675 the House of Lords held that the doctrine of frustration was capable of applying to a lease so as to bring the lease to an end when an event occurred so that no substantial use permitted by the lease and contemplated by the parties remained possible for the tenant.

5.6.5   Termination following failure to reinstate

On service of a notice to terminate following failure to rein-state, the Term is to cease absolutely but without prejudice to any rights or remedies that may have accrued to either party against the other and all money received in respect of the insurance effected by the Landlord pursuant to this Lease is to be apportioned between and paid to the Landlord and the Tenant proportionately to the market values as between a willing vendor and a willing purchaser in the market with other willing vendors and purchasers of their respective interests in the Premises immediately before the date of the damage or destruction. If the Landlord and the Tenant fail to agree on the apportionment within [   ] of the date on which this Lease is determined by a notice to terminate following failure to reinstate an independent valuer must be appointed either by agreement between the Landlord and the Tenant or in default of agreement by the President for the time being of the Royal Institution of Chartered Surveyors or his deputy or anyone nominated by him to make appointments on his behalf. The independent valuer so appointed is to act as an expert and not as an arbitrator and must determine the market values referred to in this clause ~~belong to the Landlord absolutely~~

5.6.6   Termination following damage or destruction by an uninsured Risk

If during the Term the Premises or a substantial part of them shall be damaged or destroyed by an Uninsured Risk so as to make the Premises or a substantial part of them unfit for occupation and use or inaccessible the Landlord may within one year of the date of such damage or destruction serve a notice on the Tenant confirming that it will reinstate the Premises so that the Premises shall be made fit for occupation and use or made accessible and if the Landlord fails to serve such a notice the Lease shall automatically end on the date one year after the date of such damage or destruction

5.7   *Tenant's further insurance covenants*

The Tenant covenants with the Landlord to observe and perform the requirements contained in this clause 5.7

5.7.1   Requirements of insurers

The Tenant must comply with all the reasonable requirements and recommendations of the insurers of which he has written notice

5.6.5   There has been much academic debate and some case law (*Beacon Carpets Ltd v Kirby* [1985] QB 755, CA) over the years (both inside and outside the court) as to whom insurance monies in this situation belong. On a fairly lengthy lease (eg prime retail space) there is likely to be some value in the tenant's interest and there is no sustainable reason, in the author's view, why the tenant should not benefit in some way, shape or form from the insurance monies. While the method of valuing the tenant's interest is likely to prove contentious, the principle of division of insurance monies between the parties is a fair one.

5.6.6   This amendment is made to incorporate Recommendation 8 of the Code that, if premises are damaged by an uninsured risk (as defined – see note to **clause 1.21**), the tenant should be allowed to terminate the lease unless the landlord agrees to rebuild at his own cost. The suggested new clause provides for automatic termination unless within one year the landlord elects to reinstate, which does impose a shortish time limit at the end of which the tenant knows where he stands.

5.7.1   It is unreasonable to expect a tenant to comply with requirements and recommendations of which it has no notice and which may be unreasonable either on their own account or in cost terms, and the amendments reflect these factors.

5.7.2   Policy avoidance and additional premiums

The Tenant must not knowingly do or omit anything that could |
cause any insurance policy on or in relation to the Building to
become wholly or partly void or voidable, or do or omit anything by which additional insurance premiums may become
payable unless he has previously notified the Landlord and
has agreed to pay the increased premium

5.7.3   Firefighting equipment

The Tenant must keep the Premises supplied with such fire-
fighting equipment as the insurers and, the fire authority |
require and the Landlord reasonably requires and must main- |
tain the equipment to the reasonable satisfaction of the insurers and the fire authority and in efficient working order. At
least once in every 6 months period As often as reasonably
necessary the Tenant must have the sprinkler system and |
other firefighting equipment inspected by a competent person

5.7.4   Combustible materials

The Tenant must not store on the Premises or bring onto them
anything of a specially combustible, inflammable or explosive
nature, and must comply with the requirements and recommen-
dations of the fire authority and the reasonable requirements of |
the Landlord as to fire precautions relating to the Premises

5.7.5   Fire escapes, equipment and doors

The Tenant must not obstruct the access to any fire equipment
or the means of escape from the Premises or lock any fire door
while the Premises are occupied

5.7.6   Notice of events affecting the policy

As soon as reasonably practicable after becoming aware of |
the same Tthe Tenant must give immediate notice to the
Landlord of any event of which he is aware that might affect |
any insurance policy on or relating to the Premises, and of any
event against which the Landlord may have insured under this
Lease

5.7.7   Notice of convictions

As soon as reasonably practicable after becoming aware of |
the same Tthe Tenant must give immediate notice to the |
Landlord of any conviction, judgment or finding of any court
or tribunal relating to the Tenant, or any director other officer
or major shareholder of the Tenant, of such a nature as to be
likely to affect the decision of any insurer or underwriter to
grant or to continue any insurance of the Premises |

5.7.2   This small amendment imparts the pressure of knowledge to ensure that the tenant is not strictly liable for an event or occurrence of which he is not aware.

5.7.3   The amendments here introduce the concept of reasonableness in relation to the landlord's requirements only. The final amendment brings an element of flexibility and objectivity into what otherwise is a fixed and unforgiving timetable. If the subject premises require a fire certificate then firefighting equipment must be checked once every 12 months.

5.7.4   This amendment seeks to ensure that the concept of reasonableness applies in relation to the landlord's requirements.

5.7.6   This amendment is self-explanatory. Again, without it, the strict liability imposed by the clause may work against the tenant at some future date.

5.7.7   The first amendment again avoids the imposition of a strict liability timetable. The second amendment makes the clause specific to the insurance of the premises in question.

5.7.8   Other insurance

If at any time the Tenant is entitled to the benefit of any insurance of the Premises that is not effected or maintained in pursuance of any obligation contained in this Lease, the Tenant must apply all money received by virtue of such insurance in making good the loss or damage in respect of which the money is received

5.8   *Increase or decrease of the Building*

5.8.1   Variation of the Insurance Rent Percentage

If the size of the Building is permanently increased or decreased, the Insurance Rent Percentage may be varied, if the Landlord <u>reasonably </u>so requires, with effect from the date of any consequent alteration in the Insurance Rent

5.8.2   Determination of the variation

The amount by which the Insurance Rent Percentage is varied is to be agreed by the Landlord and the Tenant or, in default of agreement within 2 months of the first proposal for variation made by the Landlord, is to be the amount the Surveyor, acting <u>reasonably and </u>as an expert and not as an arbitrator, determines to be fair and reasonable

5.9   *Landlord's Additional Insurance Covenants*

<u>The Landlord covenants with the Tenant to observe and perform the requirements set out in this clause 5.9 in relation to the insurance policy he has effected pursuant to his obligations contained in this Lease</u>

5.9.1   <u>Copy Policy</u>

<u>The Landlord must produce to the Tenant on demand a copy of the policy and the last premium renewal receipt</u>

5.9.2   <u>Noting of the Tenant's interest</u>

<u>The Landlord must ensure that the interest of the Tenant is noted or endorsed on the policy</u>

5.9.3   <u>Change of risks</u>

<u>The Landlord must notify the Tenant of any material change in the risks covered by the policy from time to time and the exclusions and excesses applicable to the policy from time to time</u>

5.8.1   The amendment proposed here introduces the concept of reasonableness into the landlord's decision to alter the percentages. An alternative would be to provide for this decision to be made by the surveyor if no clause such as **5.8.2** was included in the original draft lease.

5.8.2   In the absence of agreement on the varied Insurance Rent Percentage the ultimate arbiter will be the surveyor, acting reasonably.

5.9 (new)   This new clause imposes important obligations on the landlord very much in the interests of the tenant as it is important that the tenant's insurers or brokers have sight of both the policy (and all changes) and the relevant provisions in the lease relating to insurance so that they can advise the tenant on the cover and arrange any additional cover that the tenant may require in his own right arising out of the lease. In particular, it will be relevant to know if the policy covers the tenant's fixtures and fittings since otherwise the tenant will need to provide his own cover. See the note to clause 5 which sets out the recommendations of the Code in this respect. If the insurance is in the joint names of the landlord and the tenant or the tenant's interest is noted on the policy the waiver of subrogation referred to in **clause 5.9.4** will most likely not be needed. If not, and the tenant damages the premises through lack of care, he runs the risk of being sued by the landlord's insurer under the doctrine of subrogation (although there is case law to support the argument that when a tenant reimburses the landlord the cost of the insurance subrogation cannot apply (*Mark Rowlands Ltd v Berni Inns Ltd* [1986] QB 211, CA) but this case was expressed to turn on stated facts and cannot be regarded as fixing a principle). Clearly, however, obtaining the sort of letter referred to in **clause 5.9.4** puts the matter beyond doubt. Finally inclusion of a non-invalidation clause should be sought by the tenant and whilst there is likely to be a cost associated with this in the form of an additional premium this may well be money well spent. The tenant's insurance advisers should be involved in this debate.

5.9.4   Waiver of subrogation

The Landlord must produce to the Tenant on demand written confirmation from the insurers that they have agreed to waive all rights of subrogation against the Tenant

5.9.5   Non-Invalidation Clause

The Landlord must use reasonable endeavours to ensure that any policy effected pursuant to its obligations in this sub-clause shall contain provisions confirming that the policy cannot be made void or voidable by the Tenant or any undertenant or any other lawful occupier of the Premises or its or their representatives employers agents so that no act or omission of the Tenant or any undertenant or any other lawful occupier or its or respective employees or agents or anyone at or in the Premises with the express or implied permission of them could cause the policy to become void or voidable or render irrecoverable the whole or any part of the insurance money secured under the policy so effected

6   GUARANTEE PROVISIONS

6.1   *The Guarantor's Covenants*

6.1.1   Nature and duration

The Guarantor's covenants with the Landlord are given ~~as sole or principal debtor or covenantor,~~ with the landlord for the time being and with all his successors in title without the need for any express assignment, and the Guarantor's obligations to the Landlord will last throughout the Liability Period

6.1.2   The covenants

The Guarantor covenants with the Landlord to observe the requirements of this clause 6.1.2

6.1.2.1   Payment of rent and performance of the Lease

The Tenant must pay the Lease Rents and (upon receipt of a valid VAT invoice addressed to the Tenant for the full amount) VAT charged on them punctually and observe and perform the covenants and other terms of this Lease, and if, at any time during the Liability Period while the Tenant is bound by the tenant covenants of this Lease, the Tenant defaults in paying the Lease Rents or in observing or performing any of the covenants or other terms of this Lease, then the Guarantor must upon receipt of a valid VAT invoice addressed to the Tenant for the full amount pay the Lease Rents and observe or perform the covenants or terms in respect of which the Tenant

6 GUARANTEE PROVISIONS

Recommendation 16 of the Code: Holding former tenants and their guarantors liable: When previous tenants or their guarantors are liable to a landlord for defaults by the current tenant, landlords should notify them before the current tenant accumulates excessive liabilities. All defaults should be handled with speed and landlords should seek to assist the tenant and guarantor in minimizing losses. An assignor who wishes to remain informed of the outcome of rent reviews should keep in touch with the landlord and the landlord should provide the information. Assignors should take professional advice on what methods are open to them to minimise their losses caused by defaults by the current occupier.

It is important to consider, in the context of the requirement for a guarantor, whether as legal adviser acting on behalf of a tenant, there is any potential conflict of interest in representing a guarantor also and, if so, whether the guarantor should be told to seek independent legal advice.

See the note under the heading 'Parties' at the beginning of this book.

6.1 The deletion here ensures that the *guarantee* takes effect only as a guarantee and not as a principal indemnity. While a detailed discussion of the difference between a guarantee and an indemnity is beyond the scope of this book, briefly, a primary indemnity takes effect as a direct primary promise to pay what is owing and not simply an undertaking to pay if the tenant fails to pay. In simple terms

is in default and make good to the Landlord on demand, and indemnify the Landlord against, all reasonably foreseeable Losses resulting from such non-payment, non-performance or non-observance notwithstanding:

6.1.2.1.1 any time or indulgence granted by the Landlord to the Tenant, any neglect or forbearance of the Landlord in enforcing the payment of the Lease Rents or the observance or performance of the covenants or other terms of this Lease, or any refusal by the Landlord to accept rent tendered by or on behalf of the Tenant at a time when the Landlord is entitled (or will after the service of a notice under the Law of Property Act 1925 section 146 be entitled) to re-enter the Premises

6.1.2.1.2 that the terms of this Lease may have been varied by agreement between the Landlord and the Tenant (provided that no such variation is to bind the Guarantor to the extent that it is prejudicial to him)

6.1.2.1.3 that the Tenant has surrendered part of the Premises in which event the liability of the Guarantor under this Lease is to continue in respect of the part of the Premises not surrendered after making any necessary apportionments under the Law of Property Act 1925 section 140, and

6.1.2.1.4 anything else by which, but for this clause 6.1.2.1, the Guarantor would be released

6.1.2.2   New lease following disclaimer

If, at any time during the Liability Period while the Tenant is bound by the tenant covenants of this Lease, any trustee in bankruptcy or liquidator of the Tenant disclaims this Lease, the Guarantor must, if reasonably so required by notice served by the Landlord within 28-60 days of the Landlord's becoming aware of the disclaimer, take from the Landlord forthwith a lease of the Premises for the residue of the Contractual Term as at the date of the disclaimer, at the Rent then payable under this Lease and subject to the same covenants and terms as in this Lease the new lease to commence on the date of the disclaimer. The Guarantor must pay the reasonable and proper costs of the new lease and VAT charged thereon, save where such VAT is recoverable or available for set-off by the Landlord as input tax, and execute and deliver to the Landlord a counterpart of the new lease

6.1.2.3   Payments following disclaimer

If this Lease is disclaimed and the Landlord does not require the Guarantor to accept a new lease of the Premises in accordance with clause 6.1.2.2 NEW LEASE FOLLOWING DIS-CLAIMER, the Guarantor must pay to the Landlord on as soon

a primary indemnity puts the guarantor in a position comparable to that of an original tenant.

6.1.1   In some cases it may be appropriate for the guarantor to seek an amendment that his liability will cease after a specified number of years or, alternatively, where the tenant (more often than not where it is a company) satisfied financial tests that are specified in the lease, as one finds more frequently in Rent Deposit Deeds.

6.1.2.1   This amendment is necessary to achieve consistency with the VAT provisions inserted elsewhere throughout the lease. The final amendment removes the obligation to indemnify for reasons explained in **clause 3.14 (deleted)**.

6.1.2.1.2 It is important that any variation agreed between landlord and tenant is not prejudicial to the guarantor. While prior to the Landlord and Tenant (Covenants) Act 1995 the basic rule of law was that a guarantor would be released from his liability by any change (variation) in the principal contract (the lease) between the landlord and the tenant (except in relation to an immaterial variation or a variation for the guarantor's benefit), section 18 of the Landlord and Tenant (Covenants) Act 1995 has now altered that basic rule for a guarantor of a former tenant in respect of any relevant variation taking effect after 1 January 1995 (for either old or new leases). Now the guarantee remains in place but the Act imposes a limit on the responsibility of the guarantor of a former tenant by stripping away any liability which arises in consequence of a relevant variation. A variation is a relevant variation if the landlord, either had at the time of the variation or had immediately before the former tenant assigned the lease, an absolute right to refuse to allow it.

6.1.2.2   While the author has added the word *reasonably* it is unlikely there are going to be any circumstances when it would be unreasonable for the landlord to request this. However, there is always the remote possibility that this may be the case and this argument should be used against the landlord for its inclusion. Shortening the time period attempts to bring matters to a head so that the guarantor, at least, knows exactly where he stands within a relatively short period, ie is he going to be asked to take on board a new lease or not? The amendment relating to the costs of the new lease is self-explanatory as is the inclusion of the wording relating to VAT.

6.1.2.3   The first amendment is self-explanatory and attempts to ensure that no undue financial burden is placed on the guarantor in terms of cash flow (if nothing else), while the second obliges the landlord to bring into account any monies received in respect of the premises (ie mitigating his loss) thereby reducing the tenant's liability. The reduction of the time period from six to three months imposes a

as reasonably practicable following demand an amount equal to the difference between any money received by the Landlord for the use or occupation of the Premises and the Lease Rents for the period commencing with the date of the disclaimer and ending on whichever is the earlier of the date being 6 3 months after the disclaimer or the date, if any, upon which the Premises are relet (which the Landlord covenants to use its best endeavours to do), and the end of the Contractual Term and thereafter the Guarantor is to be released from all further liability

6.1.2.4 ~~**Guarantee of the Tenant's liabilities under an authorised guarantee agreement**~~

~~If, at any time during the Liability Period while the Tenant is bound by an authorised guarantee agreement, the Tenant makes any default in his obligations under that agreement, the Guarantor must make good to the Landlord on demand, and indemnify the Landlord against, all Losses resulting from that default notwithstanding:~~

6.1.2.4.1 ~~any time or indulgence granted by the Landlord to the Tenant, or neglect or forbearance of the Landlord in enforcing the payment of any sum or the observance or performance of the covenants of the authorised guarantee agreement~~

6.1.2.4.2 ~~that the terms of the authorised guarantee agreement may have been varied by agreement between the Landlord and the Tenant~~

6.1.2.4.3 ~~anything else by which, but for this clause 6.1.2.4, the Guarantor would be released~~

6.1.3   Severance

6.1.3.1   Severance of void provisions

Any provision of this clause 6 rendered void by virtue of the 1995 Act section 25 is to be severed from all remaining provisions, and the remaining provisions are to be preserved

6.1.3.2   Limitation of provisions

If any provision in this clause 6 extends beyond the limits permitted by the 1995 Act section 25, that provision is to be varied so as not to extend beyond those limits

6.2   *The Landlord's Covenants*

6.2.1   Notice Required

The Landlord covenants with the Guarantor that he will not attempt or be entitled to recover from the Guarantor any pay-

more reasonable period for the ongoing liability. The final amendment imposes an obligation on the landlord to mitigate his loss. Such an obligation may be unacceptable to a landlord in the context of a tenant breach and perhaps a '*reasonable endeavours*' obligation would be an acceptable compromise.

6.1.2.4   There is a healthy academic debate going on at the moment (and still unresolved) as to whether or not section 25 of the Landlord and Tenant (Covenants) Act 1995 precludes the landlord from requiring a guarantor of an original tenant or assignee under a lease to act as a guarantor of the original tenant or assignee who enters into an authorised guarantee agreement. For what it is worth it is the author's view that section 25 does preclude this requirement and, therefore, the author's view is that this clause should be deleted in its entirety, especially as the guarantor has no say in the tenant's choice of assignee. If the landlord's argument and bargaining position, however, win the day then, pending a decision of the courts on this point, the tenant's adviser should seek to ensure that similar amendments are made to this clause as those contained in **clause 6.1.2.1**.

Recommendation 15 of the Code:Varying the lease – effect on guarantors: Landlords and tenants should seek the agreement of any guarantors to any proposed material changes to the terms of the lease, or even minor changes which could increase the guarantor's liability.

6.2   This amendment is self-explanatory and, in effect, inserts as a con-
(new)   tractual obligation the provisions contained in section 27 of the Landlord and Tenant (Covenants) Act 1995.

The new clauses which have been added at **6.2.2** onwards cater for, realistically speaking, a counsel of perfection from a guarantor's

ment of any amount, determined by a court or in binding arbitration or agreed between the Landlord and the Tenant, payable in respect of a breach of covenant by the Tenant, unless he has served on the Guarantor, within 6 months of the payment being determined or agreed, a notice in the form prescribed by section 27 of the 1995 Act as if the payment were a fixed charge under that Act

6.2.2 Covenanting clause

The Landlord covenants with the Guarantor to observe and perform the provisions of this clause [ ] but so that the rights and/or remedies of the Guarantor in respect of any breach of these covenants are to be limited and extend only to a right to claim damages and not to any other right or remedy, and so that no breach of these covenants is to waive or discharge any of the Guarantor's obligations under this clause [   ]

6.2.3 Notice of the Tenant's default

6.2.3.1 If the Tenant fails to comply with any of the covenants or obligations imposed on him by this Lease other than for the payment of the rent the Landlord must serve a notice on the Tenant and the Guarantor specifying the failure ('a preliminary notice'). A preliminary notice, when served on the Tenant may but need not be accompanied by a notice served pursuant to the Law of Property Act 1925 section 146

6.2.3.2 The Landlord must serve on the Guarantor a copy of all notices served on the Tenant under section 27 of the Landlord and Tenant (Covenants) Act 1995

6.2.4 Notice that default has not been remedied or rent has not been paid

6.2.4.1 If the Tenant fails to remedy a failure specified in a preliminary notice within three months of the service of that preliminary notice and/or

6.2.4.2 the Tenant fails to pay the whole or any part of the rent or any VAT payable thereon whether or not any formal demand has been made for a period of 3 months after it has become due

the Landlord must serve a notice on the Tenant and the Guarantor ('a breach notice') specifying the failure that has not been remedied and/or the amount that has not been paid

6.2.5 No proceedings against the Guarantor without a breach notice

The Landlord must not commence any proceedings or make any claim against the Guarantor arising out of this Lease

point of view. The clauses are, largely, self explanatory and in most circumstances are highly unlikely to be accepted by the landlord. Given the nature of the proposed new clauses, it is clear to see why, in many circumstances, a tenant's obligations and those of any potential guarantor are in direct conflict. To avoid this, as stated earlier, a tenant's adviser should tell a potential guarantor to seek independent advice. If, however, any adviser finds him or herself in a position where he or she ends up acting for both the tenant and the guarantor, it is important, in the author's view, in the first instance, to at least ask for these provisions to be incorporated. Even if the landlord turns them down, a record of having asked for them on the file is likely to help should there be any problems later. This may be seen as defensive lawyering but, in the author's view, is the safest course of action.

except where the failure that has not been remedied and/or the amount that has not been paid has been specified in a properly formulated and properly given breach notice

6.2.6   Notice of late payment

The Landlord must inform the Guarantor if the Tenant is persistently late in paying the rent or any other sums due pursuant to this Lease

6.2.7   Ensuring compliance by the Tenant

The Landlord must

6.2.7.1   use all reasonable and timely endeavours to ensure compliance by the Tenant with his covenants and obligations contained in this Lease

6.2.7.2   obtain and enforce against the Tenant any remedies including forfeiture whether by re-entry or otherwise appropriate to prevent an accumulation of default and

6.2.7.3   keep the Guarantor fully informed of such endeavours and have regard to any representations or observations the Guarantor may make in respect of the Landlord's obligations contained in this clause

6.2.8   Assistance to the Guarantor

If requested by the Guarantor and at his expense the Landlord must take reasonable steps to assist the Guarantor in enforcing the Guarantor's rights against the Tenant

6.2.9   Notice of rent review negotiations

The Landlord must not initiate negotiations with the Tenant pursuant to the rent review provisions contained in this Lease or take any steps to appoint an expert pursuant to those provisions without notifying the Guarantor in writing and must keep the Guarantor fully informed of all negotiations between the Landlord and the Tenant pursuant to those provisions have proper regard to all representations or observations made by the Guarantor in that respect and if requested consent to the Guarantor becoming a party to any proceedings in connection with those provisions

6.2.10   Notice of consent to assignment

The Landlord must not give his consent to an assignment of this Lease without informing the Guarantor and having proper regard to all representations and observations that the Guarantor may make

6.3   _Assignment to the Guarantor_

If so required by the Guarantor by notice served within one month of any payment made by the Guarantor or request for payment made to him under any covenant set out under this clause [ ] the Tenant must assign the unexpired residue of the Contractual Term to the Guarantor without the payment of any premium the assignment to be completed and vacant possession of those parts of the premises then occupied by the Tenant to be given within one month of the Landlord giving his consent to the assignment under clause [ ] or a declaration from the court that the Landlord's refusal to give consent is unreasonable. Pending the completion of the assignment or if any necessary consent to the assignment is refused the Tenant must hold the unexpired residue of the Contractual Term on trust for the Guarantor

7   FORFEITURE

If and whenever during the Term:

7.1   theany undisputed Lease Rents, or any of them or any part of them, or any VAT payable on them, are is outstanding for 1428 days after becoming due, whether formally demanded or not or

7.2   the Tenant or the Guarantor materially breaches any covenant or other term of this Lease (and such breach is not remedied as soon as reasonably practicable after notice of the breach has been given) or

7.3   the Tenant or the Guarantor, being an individual, becomes bankrupt or

7   **FORFEITURE**

It may well be that landlords and their advisers are reluctant to accept any form of amendment to this particular clause but this does not mean that the tenant's adviser should not at least attempt to insert some amendments.

7.1   There may clearly be a case where rental payments (or other payments if the landlord will not accept the deletion) due under the lease are, in fact, disputed for one reason or another. The first amendment deals with that situation (disputes are unlikely to arise in relation to fixed sums which are set out in the lease or in a rent review memorandum following a review of the rent but more likely to arise in relation to service charge payments or insurance rent payments which are not fixed). Compare the definition of 'the Rent' and 'the Lease Rents' in **clause 1.34**. 'The Rent' does not include the Insurance Rent and the Service Charge, but the term 'the Lease Rents' means 'the Rent, the Insurance Rent and the Service Charge'. The second amendment ensures that any period of grace within which payment can be made (see **clause 3.17**) is consistent with the timescale set out in this clause.

7.2   The amendments here are self-explanatory. Firstly the deletion of the reference to the guarantor serves a dual purpose. Initially the tenant may well be a first-rate tenant with no problems at all, and secondly the lease may well contain a provision obliging the tenant to provide an alternative guarantor in such circumstances. In addition it prevents the landlord from harassing the tenant by instigating forfeiture proceedings for immaterial breaches. It may also be worth amending all references in the forfeiture clause to '*the Tenant*' to read '*the current tenant of the premises* …'. This would ensure that any attempt by a landlord to argue for forfeiture on the ground of, for example, liquidation of a previous corporate tenant would fail.

7.4   the Tenant ~~or the Guarantor~~, being a company, enters into liquidation whether compulsory or voluntary <u>(but not if the liquidation is for amalgamation or reconstruction of a solvent company)</u> or has a receiver appointed or

7.5   the Tenant enters into an arrangement for the benefit of his creditors or

7.6   the Tenant has any distress or execution levied on his goods <u>at the Premises which is not discharged in full within 21 days after the levy has been made</u>

and, where the Tenant ~~or the Guarantor~~ is more than one person, if and whenever any of the events referred to in this clause happens to any one or more of them the Landlord may at any time re-enter the Premises or any part of them in the name of the whole – even if any previous right of re-entry has been waived and thereupon the Term is to cease absolutely but without prejudice to any rights or remedies that may have accrued to ~~the Landlord against the Tenant or the Guarantor~~ <u>any party other than</u> in respect of any breach of covenant or other term of this Lease, including the breach in respect of which the re-entry is made <u>PROVIDED ALWAYS that in the event of there being a charge on the Lease at the time the Landlord seeks to exercise its right to forfeit the Lease and re-enter the premises, then prior to any such re-entry or the commencement of proceedings for forfeiture, the Landlord shall service notice of such proceedings or proposed re-entry on any chargee and PROVIDED FURTHER that if the Tenant (being an individual) becomes bankrupt or (being a corporate entity) enters into liquidation (whether compulsory or voluntary save for the purpose of amalgamation or reconstruction of a solvent company) or has a receiver appointed the Landlord will not exercise any rights of re-entry in consequence thereof unless neither the Tenant nor any chargee shall pay the Lease Rents reserved pursuant to the terms of this Lease in accordance with the terms of this Lease or there shall be any breach of a non-performance or non-observance of any of the other covenants or agreements on the part of the Tenant contained in this Lease</u>

7.4   There may be good corporate re-organisational reasons why it is necessary for a solvent corporate tenant to be amalgamated in some way, shape or form. The amendment inserted here prevents the landlord from using this as an opportunity to claim forfeiture of the lease.

7.6   It may well be that a third party may seek to distrain on goods as a result of a dispute that has nothing to do with the landlord and tenant relationship at this particular premises, for example where there is a dispute between the tenant and his landlord at another premises. The amendment seeks to ensure that it is only distress executed in relation to goods stored at the subject premises that will give rise to the right to forfeiture.

The final amendment preserves any accrued rights and remedies of either party against the other party or parties since the original wording only preserves the position of the landlord against the tenant and guarantor when there may well be claims by the tenant and/or the guarantor against the landlord which must also be taken into account.

Recommendation 22 of the Code: Repossession by the landlord: *Tenants threatened with repossession or whose property has been repossessed will need professional advice if they wish to try to keep or regain possession. Similarly, landlords should be clear about their rights before attempting to operate a forfeiture clause and may need professional advice.*

8   MISCELLANEOUS

8.1   *Exclusion of warranty as to use*

Nothing in this Lease or in any consent granted by the Landlord under this Lease is to imply or warrant that the Premises may lawfully be used under the Planning Acts as offices

8.2   *Representations*

The Tenant acknowledges that this Lease has not been entered into wholly or partly in reliance on any statement or representation made by or on behalf of the Landlord except any such statement or representation expressly set out in this Lease <u>and in any written or other replies made by the Landlord's Solicitors of any enquiries raised by the Tenant's solicitor</u>

8.3   *Documents under hand*

While the Landlord is a limited company or other corporation, any licence, consent, approval or notice required to be given by the Landlord ~~is to be sufficiently given if given under the hand of a director, the secretary or other duly authorised officer of the Landlord or by the Surveyor on behalf of the Landlord~~<u>must be given as a deed properly executed by the Landlord</u>

8.4   *Tenant's property*

If, after the Tenant has vacated the Premises at the end of the Term any property of his remains in or on the Premises and he fails to remove it within ~~7~~<u>14</u> days after a written request from the Landlord to do so or, if the Landlord is unable to make such a request to the Tenant<u> despite having used his best endeavours so to do</u>, within ~~14~~<u>28</u> days from the first attempt to make one, then the Landlord may sell that property as the agent of the Tenant. ~~The Tenant must indemnify the Landlord against any liability incurred by the Landlord to any third party whose property is sold by him in the mistaken belief held in good faith — which is to be presumed unless the contrary is proved — that the property belonged to the Tenant.~~ If, having used <u>its best</u>~~made reasonable~~ efforts to do so, the Landlord is unable to locate the Tenant, then the Landlord may retain the proceeds of sale absolutely unless the Tenant claims them within 6 months of the date upon which he vacated the Premises. ~~The Tenant must indemnify the Landlord against any damage occasioned to the Premises and any losses caused by or related to the presence of the property in or on the Premises~~

8   MISCELLANEOUS

8.2   This is a standard amendment familiar to conveyancers in any form of property-based contractual relationship and it is unlikely to prove to be contentious.

8.3   If the landlord is a corporate body then there should be no room for dispute as to whether the signatory to a document has been duly authorised or whether for any other reason the document has been validly executed. This amendment seeks to avoid this. While there may be delays occasioned by relevant signatories etc not being available, it is far preferable to have a delay prior to execution of the documentation rather than problems later if the landlord so seeks to argue that the document executed under hand was signed by an individual who did not have the requisite authority.

8.4   From the tenant's point of view, ideally this entire clause should be deleted. It is unlikely that any tenant is going to disappear completely without trace. A corporate tenant is nearly always traceable either through a liquidator, receiver or other officers although, admittedly, it may be more difficult with individuals who choose for whatever reasons to go missing. In any event, if the goods belong to the tenant then the landlord should try to return them. However, a landlord is not likely to want to be in a position whereby at the end of the term he cannot relet the premises because the previous tenant's goods are still located there. If deletion of the whole clause proves to be unacceptable the suggested amendments should be sought. The time periods are self-explanatory as is the provision imposing an obligation on the landlord to try and locate the tenant. The reason for deletion of the indemnities has been discussed in **clause 3.12.1.**

8.5   *Compensation on vacating excluded*

~~Any statutory right of the Tenant to claim compensation from the Landlord on vacating the Premises is excluded to the extent that the law allows~~

8.6   *Notices*

8.6.1   Form and service of notices

A notice under this Lease must be in writing and, unless the receiving party or his <u>authorised</u> agent acknowledges receipt, is valid if, and only if:

8.6.1.1   it is given by hand, sent by registered post or recorded delivery~~, or sent by fax provided a confirmatory copy is given by hand or sent by registered post or recorded delivery on the same day~~ and

8.6.1.2   it is served:

8.6.1.2.1   where the receiving party is a company incorporated within Great Britain, at the registered office

8.6.1.2.2   where the receiving party is the Tenant and the Tenant is not such a company, at the Premises and

8.6.1.2.3   where the receiving party is the Landlord or the Guarantor and that party is not such a company, at that party's address shown in this Lease or at any address specified in a notice given by that party to the other parties <u>PROVIDED ALWAYS that for so long as this lease remains vested in [the original tenant] any notice served on the Tenant shall be served at its registered office and not at the Premises</u>

8.6.2   Deemed delivery

8.6.2.1   By registered post or recorded delivery

~~Unless it is returned through the Royal Mail undelivered,~~ a notice sent by registered post or recorded delivery is <u>not</u> to be treated as served on the 2nd working day after posting whenever, and whether or not, it is received<u> nor shall section 23 of the Landlord and Tenant Act 1927 apply to the Lease</u>

~~8.6.2.2   By fax~~

~~A notice sent by fax is to be treated as served on the day on which it is sent, or the next working day where the fax is sent after 1600 hours or on a day that is not a working day, whenever and whether or not it or the confirmatory copy is received unless the confirmatory copy is returned through the Royal Mail undelivered~~

8.5   If there has been a change of ownership of the lease during the last
           five years of the contractual term and any assignee is *not* a succes-
           sor to the business of the assignor (and possibly previous occupier)
           the landlord is able, contractually, in the lease to deny statutory
           compensation to the tenant. The author regards this as unsustain-
           able from the landlord's point of view and should be strenuously
           resisted by the tenant. Such a provision as originally drafted may
           affect marketability of the lease in its last five years.

8.6.1   Insertion of the word '*authorised*' seeks to ensure that there is no dis-
           pute as to whether or not the party acknowledging receipt of the
           notice had the necessary authority to do so.

8.6.1.1   There is always a potential debate as to whether or not a notice sent
           by fax has in fact actually been received and, if received, what has
           been done with it at the receiving address. Was it brought to the
           attention of the appropriate person? Was it simply left on someone's
           desk date stamped and then mislaid? It is better to be safe and pro-
           vide for more traditional methods of service.

8.6.1.2.3 This amendment is self-explanatory and ensures that important
           notices are not simply left at the premises and deemed to be unim-
           portant! An amendment like the one suggested makes service at the
           tenant's registered office mandatory and not down to the whim of
           the landlord (*Claire's Accessories UK Ltd v Kensington High Street
           Associates Ltd* (2001) unreported).

8.6.2.1   The tenant should consider deleting the whole of this clause since
           the risk of non-delivery is placed on the recipient. Further, it should
           be noted that section 23(1) of the Landlord and Tenant Act 1927
           (which deals with the service of notices under the Landlord and
           Tenant Act 1954 and the Landlord and Tenant (Covenants) Act
           1995) imposes a presumption of service if the notice is (inter alia)
           sent by registered post or recorded delivery. The cases of *Blunden v
           Frogmore Investments Limited* [2002] 20 EG 223 and *Webber
           (Transport) Limted v Railtrack plc* [2003] EWCA Civ 166 illustrate
           the very considerable dangers to the tenant, who should therefore
           seriously consider excluding the operation of section 23 of the
           Landlord and Tenant Act 1927 as well as deleting **clause 8.6.2.1.**
           Hence the suggested amendments to this clause.

8.6.2.2   The same comments apply here as that referred to in **clause 8.6.1.1**
           above.

8.6.2.3   'A working day'

References to 'a working day' are references to a day when the majority of the United Kingdom clearing banks are open for business in the City of London

8.6.3   Joint recipients

If the receiving party consists of more than one person, a notice to one of them is notice to all

8.7   *Rights and easements*

The operation of the Law of Property Act 1925 section 62 is excluded from this Lease and the only rights granted to the Tenant are those expressly set out in this Lease and the Tenant is not to be entitled to any other rights affecting any adjoining property of the Landlord

8.8   *Covenants relating to adjoining property*

~~The Tenant is not to be entitled to the benefit of or the right to enforce or to prevent the release or modification of any covenant agreement or condition entered into by any tenant of the Landlord in respect of any adjoining property of the Landlord~~

8.9   *Disputes with adjoining occupiers*

If any dispute arises between the Tenant and the tenants or occupiers of any adjoining property of the Landlord in connection with the Premises and any of that adjoining property, it is to be decided by the ~~Landlord~~ Surveyor acting as an expert and not as an arbitrator or in such other manner as the Landlord reasonably directs

8.10   *Effect of waiver*

~~Each of the Tenant's covenants is to remain in full force both at law and in equity even if the Landlord has waived or released that covenant, or waived or released any similar covenant affecting any adjoining property of the Landlord~~ PROVIDED ALWAYS that this clause shall only have effect in relation to a demand for and acceptance of rent during such period as may be reasonable for enabling the parties hereto to carry on negotiations for remedying the said breach once the Landlord or its agent have received notice of it

8.11   *The perpetuity period*

The perpetuity period applicable to this Lease is 80 years from the commencement of the Contractual Term, and whenever in

8.6.2.3   The amendment here is self-explanatory.

8.8   Consideration should be given as to whether this clause should be deleted by the tenant's adviser after ascertaining whether such covenants exist and, if so, does the tenant need the benefit of them. There are only a limited set of circumstances in which one tenant may be able to enforce a covenant against another (a building scheme, a letting scheme, where tenants (or their predecessors) have entered into a mutual deed of covenant or where a tenant has taken an assignment of the benefit of a covenant from the landlord) and it is unlikely a commercial lease will fall into any of these categories. If the landlord insists that the clause remains, a proviso should be added at the end as follows, '... *provided always that the Premises are not adversely affected thereby*'.

8.9   The amendment provides an element of professional expertise is brought to bear and the concept of reasonableness is introduced in any such disputes. The tenant needs to be aware that this clause may restrict any independent action it may wish to take against another tenant and the tenant may wish to see this clause deleted. It will only be enforceable, if it remains, if the other tenant who is party to the dispute has a similar provision in his clause.

8.10   This clause attempts to get round the harsh application of the law of waiver. As the law stands at present it is the author's view that this clause is void and should be deleted.

8.11   The amendment at the end of the clause spells out the effect of a failure of a future right to vest within the perpetuity period.

this Lease any party is granted a future interest it must vest within that period <u>or be void for remoteness</u>

8.12   *Exclusion of liability*

~~The Landlord is not to be responsible to the Tenant or to any one at the Premises or the Estate expressly or by implication with the Tenant's authority for any accident happening or injury suffered or for any damage to or loss of any chattel sustained in the Premises or on the Estate~~ PROVIDED ALWAYS that this clause shall not be construed as relieving the Landlord from liability for breach by the Landlord of any of the covenants contained in this lease and shall be construed as if the provisions of the Unfair Contract Terms Act 1977 applied to this clause

8.13   *New lease*

This lease is a new tenancy for the purposes of the 1995 Act section 1

8.14   *Agreement for lease*

It is certified that there is no agreement for lease to which this documents gives effect

8.15   *Exclusion of the 1954 Act ss 24–28*

8.15.1   Notice and declaration

On [   ] the Landlord served notice on the Tenant pursuant to the provisions of the 1954 Act Section 38A(3) as inserted by the Regulatory Reform (Business Tenancies) (England and Wales) Order 2003 and on [ ] the Tenant made a [simple *(or as appropriate)* statutory] declaration pursuant to schedule 2 of the Regulatory Reform (Business Tenancies) (England and Wales) Order 2003

8.15.2   Agreement to exclude

Pursuant to the provisions of the 1954 Act Section 38A(1) as inserted by the Regulatory Reform (Business Tenancies) (England and Wales) Order 2003 the parties agree that the provisions of the 1954 Act Sections 24–28 inclusive are to be excluded in relation to the tenancy created by this Lease.]

8.12   The author would press for this clause to be deleted in its entirety. It is not possible to *contract out* of liability for negligence resulting in personal injury, or death and the tenant should argue that the clause should be deleted on this basis. Alternatively, the tenant's adviser should seek to turn it around and impose a reciprocal exclusion on the landlord so that neither party is responsible to the other for the consequences of any of the matters set out in this clause and then leave it for the courts to decide the extent to which such exclusions are effective.

8.14   It is always worthwhile checking to ensure that there is in fact no such agreement for lease which may need to be stamped. It can quite often be overlooked especially when there is a long period between exchange of agreements for lease and completion of the lease and it is worth remembering the circumstances in which it is necessary to pay stamp duty on the agreement for lease as opposed to the lease document itself. (See section 240 of the Finance Act 1994.)

8.15   Is the lease to be contracted out of the security of tenure provisions of the Landlord and Tenant Act 1954? If not, this clause should be deleted.

The Regulatory Form (Business Tenancies) (England and Wales) Order 2003 abolished the need for the parties to apply to the court for a consent order. The change with effect from 1 June 2004 was its replacement by a two-tier approach with a normal and an accelerated procedure which only applies 'in relation to a tenancy to be granted for a term of years certain' and enables the parties to agree to exclude the security provisions of the Landlord and Tenant Act 1954 if the landlord has served on the tenant 'a notice in the form, or substantially in the form' set out in Schedule 1 of the 2003 Order (commonly referred to as the 'health warning notice'), and the requirements specified in Schedule 2 of the 2003 Order are met. The alternatives are twofold. First the advance notice procedure is followed where the health warning notice must be served on the tenant 'not less than 14 days before the tenant enters into the tenancy......... or (if earlier) becomes contractually bound to do so,' and then the tenant must, before entering into the tenancy or becoming contractually bound to do so, 'make a declaration in the form, or substantially in the form' set out in paragraph 7 of Schedule 2 of the 2003 Order (a 'simple declaration'). Secondly, the statutory declaration procedure is followed where the health warning notice is served on the tenant less than 14 days before the tenant enters into the tenancy or becomes contractually bound to do

8.16   *Exclusion of the 1954 Act Sections 24–28 in relation to lease to Guarantor*

8.16.1   **Notice and declaration**

On [   ]   the Landlord served notice on the Guarantor pursuant to the provisions of

so, in which case, instead of the simple declaration under the normal procedure, the tenant must before entering into the tenancy or becoming contractually bound to do so 'make a statutory declaration in the form, or substantially in the form' set out in paragraph 8 of Schedule 2 of the 2003 Order. In the case of both the normal and accelerated procedure a reference to the notice and declaration (whether a simple declaration or a statutory declaration) must be 'contained in or endorsed' on the lease and the agreement to exclude the security provisions or reference to the agreement, must be 'contained in or endorsed' on the lease.

It should be appreciated that failure to follow the procedures will render the exclusion agreement 'void' and the tenant will retain the statutory right to renew. Note also that it only applies, as before, to 'a tenancy granted for a term of years certain', and it is not applicable to periodic tenancies. The only details required in the warning notice are the names and addresses of the tenant and the landlord. Details of the premises demised are not required, but it may be sensible to insert this in the form and also have the notice signed by the landlord's solicitor for and on behalf of the landlord, and finally to date this so that it will be possible in the future to check that 14 days elapsed between the warning notice being served and the tenant becoming contractually bound where the normal procedure is followed.

The question, therefore, will have to be addressed whether a fresh notice and declaration, whether a simple declaration or a statutory declaration, will be required if subsequently the terms of the lease are amended following service of the health warning notice but before completion. In *Receiver for the Metropolitan Police District v Palacegate Properties Ltd* (2000) 13 EG 187 which concerned a subsequent change in the lease terms under the old law, the court held that lease granted had to be in 'substantially' the same form as the draft submitted to the court. It is suggested that the position is likely to remain unchanged.

The position of the guarantor as a potential protected tenant has been overlooked since if the lease is contracted out the landlord will want to ensure that a lease taken by the guarantor is likewise contracted out. The warning notice and declaration procedure should therefore be operated with the guarantor before he becomes a party to the lease. Likewise in the case of option to renew a lease the warning notice and declaration procedure should be operated before the lease is entered into.

8.16   A break clause for the tenant will have been agreed by negotiation. Break clauses have become ever more popular in recent years as facilitating tools to enable lease terms to be agreed. Up until about five years ago, the accepted commercial compromise when negotiating break clauses on behalf of a tenant was to delete an absolute covenant compliance precondition and, if the landlord insisted on some form of compliance precondition, to accept a *material* compli-

the 1954 Act Section 38A(3) as inserted by the Regulatory Reform (Business Tenancies) (England and Wales) Order 2003 relating to the tenancy to be entered into by the Guarantor pursuant to clause 6.1.2.2 and on [   ] the Guarantor made a [simple *(or as appropriate)* statutory] declaration pursuant to schedule 2 of the Regulatory Reform (Business Tenancies) (England and Wales) Order 2003

8.16.2   Agreement to exclude

Pursuant to the provisions of the 1954 Act Section 38A(1) as inserted by the Regulatory Reform (Business Tenancies) (England and Wales) Order 2003 the parties agree that the provisions of the 1954 Act Sections 24–28 inclusive are to be excluded in relation to any tenancy entered into by the Guarantor pursuant to clause 6.1.2.2]

8.17   *Tenant's break clause*

If the Tenant wishes to determine this lease on the day of and shall give to the Landlord not less than [ ] months notice in writing and shall up to the time of such determination pay the

ance or *reasonable performance* obligation in relation to those covenants.

The case of *Reed Personnel Services plc v American Express Ltd* [1997] 1 EGLR 229 was a case in point where the Courts had to interpret a precondition to a break option requiring reasonable performance of *tenant's covenants*. This case turned on the interpretation of the repairing obligation. The judge threw out the tenant's arguments that certain breaches of covenant were not serious because they were essentially decorative. The Judge was unswayed and argued that any precondition, trivial or otherwise, must be complied with, and that reasonable steps should have been taken by the tenants to comply. Whilst it was not necessary for the tenant to have performed their obligations to the letter, they had to show at least a degree of compliance and, therefore, the tenant lost out. Therefore, the clear and unequivocal advice to anyone advising a tenant has to be not to accept *any* form of covenant compliance precondition. This also extends to payment of rent and any other sums due under the lease. The landlord has many remedies for failure by the tenant to pay and the case of *Credit Lyonnais v Russell Jones & Walker* [2002] EWHL 1310 highlights that a failure to pay on time can be catastrophic for a tenant. If the tenant has breached any of the covenants which have resulted in a loss to the landlord, then the landlord has other appropriate remedies available to it.

The second amendment to the clause is self explanatory. Why should only antecedent breaches by the tenant (as opposed to the landlord) survive? Finally in the absence of any contractual provision to the contrary any rent paid in advance by the tenant for any period beyond the contractual break date does not fall to be apportioned and therefore cannot be recovered by the tenant. See *William Hill (Football) Ltd v Willen Key and Hardware Ltd* [1964] 190 EG 867. The final amendment seeks to counter this point and put the issue beyond doubt, albeit that the landlord will no doubt argue for its retention and possible set-off against any terminal dilapidations claim!

Recommendation 23 of the Code: Renewals under the Landlord and Tenant Act 1954: *The parties should take professional advice on the Landlord and Tenant Act 1954 and the PACT scheme at least six months before the end of the term of the lease and also immediately upon receiving any notice under the Act from the other party or their agent. Guidance on the Act can be found in the Department for Transport, Local Government and the Regions, 'Guide to the Landlord and Tenant Act 1954' (see inside back-cover).*

8.17   An option by which the tenant can renew the lease may become increasingly common as the trend continues for lease terms to be reduced, partly driven by a wish to minimise the stamp duty land tax at the outset and the trouble and expense of registering a lease for more than seven years at HM Land Registry with the lease then

rent reserved by and perform and observe the covenants contracted in this Lease then upon the expiry of such notice the Term shall immediately cease and determine but without prejudice to any rights the Landlord either party may have against the Tenant other for any antecedent breach PROVIDED ALWAYS that upon such determination the Landlord shall forthwith repay to the Tenant any Lease Rents paid in advance for any period applicable to any period beyond the date of such determination

8.18   *Option to renew*

8.18.1   Grant and exercise of the option

If the Tenant wishes to take a further lease of the Premises from the end of the Contractual Term, and at any time after the end of the   ] year of the Contractual Term gives to the Landlord [not less than] [   ] notice of that wish, then, [provided the Tenant has paid the Lease Rents] up to the end of the Contractual] Term, the Landlord must grant to the Tenant a further lease of the

being generally available for public inspection unless commercially sensitive information has been edited out in consequence of the lease being designated as an exempt information document. For example, rather than taking a ten-year lease with an option to determine this at the end of five years, a tenant may seek to restructure the lease as an initial five-year term with an option to renew for a further five years. The option to renew automatically passes to the respective successors in title of the landlord and tenant, subject to questions of registration.

An option to renew a lease may be conditional, for example, arising only if the tenant has complied with various preconditions such as exercising the option by notice in writing to the landlord on or before a fixed date and possibly subject to compliance with the covenants in the lease which will be construed strictly. As with a break clause in a lease a tenant should resist preconditions or qualify them as best it can. A requirement of strict compliance with the covenants is very likely to thwart a tenant in seeking to exercise an option to renew a lease as is the case with break clauses in leases. The option will need to provide a mechanism for determining the rent to be paid under the renewed lease since without this the option may be void for uncertainty. Also the option should provide that the terms of the new lease exclude the option to renew since otherwise this operates as a perpetually renewable lease. If there is a formula but no machinery specified for settling the new rent, the court has been prepared to apply the formula so that the absence of any machinery is not fatal. Similarly, if the machinery for settling the new rent breaks down the courts have been prepared to substitute its own.

It is important that option is registered as a notice or restriction on the landlord's title if registered or as a C(iv) land charge if the landlord's title is unregistered. If the landlord's title is registered, then provided the tenant is in actual occupation the option may be enforceable as an overriding interest against a purchaser of the reversion. If the landlord's title is unregistered the failure to register the option renders it void against a purchaser of the legal estate from the landlord for money or money's worth, although the principle of either a constructive trust or estoppel may result in the option being binding.

8.18 The landlord may well wish to exclude the application of the doctrine of a 'letting scheme'. In *Williams v Kiley* [2002] EWCA Civ 1645 the Court held that the doctrine of a letting scheme applied to the units within a shopping arcade. One tenant was therefore able directly to enforce the user covenant in a neighbour's lease without the landlord's assistance as the lease demonstrated an intention to create rights enforceable by the lessees themselves against each other without the need for the landlord's involvement.

Premises for a term of [   ]
years commencing on and including the day following the last
day of the Contractual Term, on the same terms and conditions
as this Lease except as to the Initial Rent, the Review Dates
and this option for a further lease.

8.18.2   The rent under the new lease

The initial rent reserved by the further lease is to be an
amount equal to the rent payable under this Lease at the end
of the Contractual Term, and the review dates under the further
lease are to be *(specify the review dates or method of identi-
fying them)*

8.18.3   Registration of the option

(version 1)

[The Option is to be of no effect if the Tenant fails to register
it as a land charge under the Land Charges Act 1972 within
[   ] from the date of this document.]
(use where reversion unregistered)

(version 2)

[The Option is to be of no effect if the Tenant fails to protect it
by notice in the register of the Landlord's title under the Land
Registration Act 2002 within [   ]
from the date of this document.] *(use where reversion registered)*

8.19   *Exclusion of Liability*

The Landlord shall not be liable to observe or perform any
obligation on its part contained in this Lease (and the Tenant
hereby releases the Landlord from time to time from all liability in respect of any breach or non observance of any such
obligation) after it has ceased to be entitled to the immediate
reversion expectant upon the Term

8.20   *Data Protection Act 1998*

For the purposes of the Data Protection Act 1998 or otherwise
the Tenant and the Guarantor (if any) acknowledge that information relating to this tenancy will be held on computer and
other filing systems by the Landlord or the Landlord's managing agent (if any) for the purposes of general administration
and/or enforcement of this Lease and agree to such information being used for such purposes and being disclosed to third
parties so far only as is necessary in connection with the management of the Landlord's interest in, the insurance and/or
maintenance of the Premises, checking the creditworthiness of

the Tenant and the Guarantor, or the disposal or subletting of the Premises of the Building of which the Premises form part, or is necessary to confirm with recognised industry practice in the management and letting of property

8.21   *Third party rights and the Contracts (Rights of Third Parties) Act 1999*

For the avoidance of doubt nothing in this Lease shall confer on any third party any benefit or the right to enforce any term of this Lease and without prejudice to the generality of the foregoing the Contracts (Rights of Third Parties) Act 1999 shall not apply to this Lease. [Nor is it intended by the parties to this Lease to create a building scheme]

IN WITNESS whereof the parties hereto have executed this lease as a deed on the date first hereinbefore written

SCHEDULE 1 – THE PREMISES

The expression 'the Premises' includes those parts of the Building shown edged red on the Plans 2, 3 and 4 and the Included Car Parking Bays shown coloured green on Plan 1 but excludes the roof and the roof space, the foundations, and all external, structural or loadbearing walls, columns, beams and supports [*(or as required in the circumstances)*] including:

1. the paint paper and other decorative finishes applied to the interior of the external walls and columns of the Building but not any other part of the external walls and columns

2. the floor finishes but nothing below them

3. the ceiling finishes and any suspended ceilings but nothing above the ceiling finishes

4. any non-load-bearing internal walls wholly within the Premises

5. the inner half of the internal non-load-bearing walls dividing the Premises from other parts of the Building

6. the door and windows and the door and window frames

7. all additions and improvements

8. all fittings installed by the Landlord

9. all fixtures (whether or not fixed to the Premises at the commencement of the Term) except any installed by the Tenant that can be removed without defacing the Premises

10. any Conducting Media wholly in the Premises that exclusively serve the Premises

SCHEDULE 1 – THE PREMISES

When only part of a building is being leased, it is absolutely vital to clearly identify the extent of the building which comprises the premises since, most critically, the tenant's repairing obligation will only extend to the premises (as defined) as will all the other obligations of the tenant. As the requirements are in respect of a plan see LRR 2003 r213 as referred to in the note to **clause 1.34**. Coupled with this, it is also vital for the tenant's adviser to look at the definition of the premises in conjunction with the definition of *Retained Parts* (see **clause 1.36**), since by virtue of **clause 4.2.1** the landlord is obliged to use his best endeavours to provide the services and these include (in paragraph 2.11.1 of Schedule 6 (as amended)) the repair, replacement, renewal and decoration of the Retained Parts. What must be absolutely avoided is a situation where essential repairs which are not the tenant's responsibility are also not clearly the express obligation of the landlord since a situation could then arise where the responsibility for the repairs does not lie with either party. In *Adami v Lincoln Grange Management Ltd* [1998] 1 EGLR 58, the Court of Appeal held that no principle could be discerned which requires the implication on the part of a landlord to keep the structure of a building in good repair when the lease was silent on this point. While the maxim *contra proferentem* will apply against the person offering it (ie the landlord), it is not good practice to leave it to the courts to decide, most likely only after expensive litigation, where relative liabilities lie! Further it should be noted that a most unsatisfactory position can occur when neither party is legally liable to carry out essential repairs in consequence of a vacuum left in the repairing obligations under the lease. In *Credit Suisse v Beegas Nominees Limited* [1994] All ER 803 the court accepted that parties to a lease may leave a gap in their obligations. This critical black hole is often encountered where the tenant's repairing obligation is modified by reference to a Schedule of Condition without the landlord agreeing to accept responsibility for the defects in the premises recorded in the Schedule of Condition. The tenant should seek to impose an obligation on the landlord to be responsible for these. The detailed definition of the premises should ensure that this does not happen. What is also absolutely imperative is that if a survey is undertaken (something the author strongly recommends *if* only for someone to have the opportunity to inspect the site and identify works that the tenant may require the landlord to carry out either as a precondition to taking the lease or with which to negotiate a rent-free period) and if there are any unusual features of the building the surveyor should be asked to give his view as to who should have the responsibility of repair and maintenance of these items.

In leases which comprise entire buildings, without any express provision to the contrary, both the sub-soil beneath and air space above would be included in the premises unless otherwise expressly excluded. These may be valuable assets or impose burdensome liabilities which both parties will need to consider.

SCHEDULE 2 – THE RIGHTS GRANTED

1   Right to use the common parts

The right, subject to temporary interruption for repair, alter- |
ation, rebuilding or replacement, for the Tenant and all persons expressly or by implication authorised by him, in
common with the Landlord and all other persons having a like
right, to use appropriate areas of the Common Parts for all
proper purposes in connection with the use and enjoyment of
the Premises at such times as they are open in accordance
with the Landlord's obligations in this Lease

2   Passage and running through the adjoining conduits

The right, subject to temporary interruption for repair, alter- |
ation or replacement, to the free passage and running of all
services which now or at any time during the Term run through |
the appropriate Adjoining Conduits, in common with the
Landlord and all other persons having a like right together |
with the right at reasonable times and on reasonable prior
notice (save in emergency where no notice need be given) to
have access to other parts of the Building for the purposes of
maintenance and repair of the same

3   Display of nameplates or signs

The right to have two nameplates or signs displayed in positions on the outside of the Building adjacent to its main
entrance and in the reception area of the Building, of sizes to
be specified by the Landlord (acting reasonably) showing the |
Tenant's name and any other details approved by the Landlord
such approval not to be unreasonably withheld or delayed and
PROVIDED ALWAYS that nothing in this paragraph or anywhere else in this lease shall preclude the Tenant from displaying its usual corporate or trade logo

4   Right to use the additional parking bays

4.1   The right to use the Additional Parking Bays or such other car
parking bays as the Landlord from time to time reasonably |
designates in writing

5   Support

The rights of light air support protection shelter and all other |
easements and rights at the date of this Lease belonging to or
enjoyed by the Premises

SCHEDULE 2 – THE RIGHTS GRANTED

1   The amendment here provides that any interruption in the right to use common parts is only a temporary interruption.

2   The first amendment achieves the same purpose as that referred to at **paragraph 2.1** above. The second amendment ensures the tenant has the right to use any *services* which are installed at a future date, while the final amendment ensures that if it is necessary for whatever reason for the tenant to need to repair an Adjoining Conduit (eg landlord default) the necessary right exists to go into other parts of the building (including other areas constructed for letting) to carry out the repair and/or maintenance.

3   The first amendment once again introduces an element of reasonableness into the process of obtaining landlord's approval as to the specification for the signs etc. The second amendment (perhaps more importantly for the tenant) precludes the landlord from objecting to the tenant's usual trade insignia. The tenant's trade insignia is likely to be known to the landlord and this proviso enables the tenant to proceed without delay in exhibiting the nameplate or sign. (See **clause 3.6.2**.)

4   The amendment once again introduces the concept of reasonableness into the landlord's decision-making process.

5   This amendment incorporates self-explanatory rights which are simply a reciprocation of those contained in **paragraph 5** of Schedule 3.

6   EMERGENCY ACCESS

The right in the case of emergency of access through any adjoining or neighbouring parts of the Building

6   This right would be exercisable in the event of fire or any other emergency and is self-explanatory.

SCHEDULE 3 – THE RIGHTS RESERVED

<u>All rights reserved in this Schedule are subject to the provisions of clause 4.4:</u>

1   PASSAGE AND RUNNING THROUGH THE CONDUITS

1.1   The right to the free and uninterrupted passage and running of all appropriate services or supplies from and to other parts of the Building or any adjoining property of the Landlord in and through the Conduits and through any structures of a similar use or nature that may at any time be in over or under the Premises

2   CONSTRUCTION OF CONDUITS

~~2.1   The right to construct and to maintain at any time any pipes, sewers, drains, mains, ducts, conduits, gutters, watercourses, wires, cables, laser optical fibres, data or impulse transmission, communication or reception systems, channels, flues and other necessary conducting media for the provision of services or supplies, including any fixings, louvres, cowls and any other ancillary apparatus for the benefit of any other part of the Building or any of the Adjoining Property~~

3   ACCESS

3.1   *Access to inspect*

3.1.1   The right at any time to enter, or in emergency to break into and enter, the Premises ~~at any time during the Term~~ <u>at reasonable times on reasonable notice except in emergency</u>

3.1.1.1   to inspect the condition and the state of repair of the Premises

3.1.1.2   to inspect, clean, connect with, repair, remove, replace with others, alter or execute any works whatever to or in connection with the conduits, easements, supplies or services referred to in paragraphs 1 and 2 <u>where such viewing or work would not otherwise be reasonably practicable</u>

3.1.1.3   to view the state and condition of and repair and maintain the Building <u>where such viewing or work would not otherwise be reasonably practicable</u>

SCHEDULE 3 – THE RIGHTS RESERVED

The additional introductory wording, which is a qualification of all the rights reserved, ensures that the amendment which the tenant will hopefully have negotiated in **clause 4.4 (new)** applies in relation to the exercise of all rights reserved to the landlord which involve entry onto the premises. Such rights could be immensely disruptive to a tenant and a landlord would have difficulty in objecting to such a precondition.

2.1   This right, if included and then exercised by a landlord, could be hugely disruptive to a tenant and could make beneficial occupation by the tenant virtually untenable. It should be deleted in its entirety. Then, if the landlord wishes to undertake any of the works envisaged, some form of licence outside the scope of the lease would have to be negotiated.

3.1   The amendment is self explanatory.

3.1.1.2   The amendment ensures that, if it is reasonably practicable for the landlord to undertake the specified works without interrupting the tenant's occupation then the landlord should have no rights of access.

3.1.1.3   This amendment achieves the same purpose as the amendment to **paragraph 3.1.1.2** above and seeks to ensure that if it is practicable for the landlord to exercise any of these rights without interrupting the tenant's beneficial occupation access will be denied.

3.1.1.4   to carry out work or do anything whatever that the Landlord is obliged to do under this Lease <u>where such viewing or work would not otherwise be reasonably practicable</u>

3.1.1.5   to take schedules or inventories of fixtures and other items to be yielded up at the end of the Term and

3.1.1.6   to exercise any of the rights granted to the Landlord by this Lease

~~3.2~~   ~~Access on renewal or rent review~~

~~The right with the Surveyor and any person acting as the third party determining the Rent in default of agreement under the provisions for rent review contained in this Lease at any time to enter and to inspect and measure the Premises for all purposes connected with any pending or intended step under the 1954 Act or the implementation of the provisions for rent review~~

4   SCAFFOLDING

The right to <u>temporarily </u>erect scaffolding for any <u>proper </u>purpose connected with or related to the Building ~~even if it~~<u>but only if the same does not</u> restrict~~s~~ access to or the use and enjoyment of the Premises

5   SUPPORT

The rights of light, air, support, protection, shelter and all other easements and rights at the date of this Lease belonging to or enjoyed by other parts of the Building

6   RIGHT TO ERECT NEW BUILDINGS

6.1   Full right and liberty at any time after the date of this Lease:

6.1.1   to alter, raise the height of, or rebuild the Building, which expression here includes the Premises and

6.1.2   to erect any new buildings of any height on any adjoining property of the Landlord in such manner as the Landlord thinks fit even if they may obstruct, affect, or interfere with the amenity of or access to the Premises or the passage of light and air to the Premises, ~~and even~~<u>but only</u> if they <u>do not </u>affect the Premises or their use and enjoyment

3.1.1.4   See **paragraphs 3.1.1.2** and **3.1.1.3** above.

3.2   This clause should be deleted in its entirety. The lease renewal or rent review procedures may place the parties in adversarial roles so that the tenant will not welcome such an opportunity for the landlord to cause disruption and potential embarrassment. In any event, **paragraph 3.1.1.1** should contain the necessary rights for the landlord and should be sufficient for any legitimate inspection purpose. The landlord should have all the premises' dimensions and measurements available from the outset of the lease so that he is in a position to conduct the rent reviews as and when they occur. Having given up possession of the premises to the tenant for the contractual term granted by the lease the tenant should be entitled to exclusive possession and therefore to rely on these arguments for deleting this clause.

4   The first amendment is self-explanatory, while the second amendment places a restriction on the exercise of the right so that the erection of scaffolding does not interfere with the tenant's use of the premises. There is absolutely no reason why the tenant should accept any scaffolding which interferes with his occupation which may, in any event, amount to a breach of the landlord's covenant for quiet enjoyment. If it does, then he should argue that there ought to be some sort of reduction in the rent together with payment of compensation while the obstruction subsists. Refer in this connection to *Speiro Lechoritis v Goldmile Properties Limited* [2003] 125 EG 143 referred to in the note to **clause 4.1**.

6.1.2   The same arguments apply here as those referred to in **paragraph 4** above. A compromise for the tenant would be to insert the word 'materially' before the word 'affect' in the last line of this clause.

SCHEDULE 4 – THE RENT AND RENT REVIEW

1   DEFINITIONS

For all purposes of this schedule the terms defined in this paragraph 1 have the meanings specified

1.1   *'An arbitrator'*

References to 'an arbitrator' are references to a person appointed by agreement between the Landlord and the Tenant or, in the absence of agreement within 14 days of one of them giving notice to the other of his nomination, nominated by the President on the application of either made not earlier than 6 months before the relevant review date or at any time there-after to determine the rent under this schedule

1.2   **'The Assumptions'**

'The Assumptions' means:

SCHEDULE 4 – THE RENT AND RENT REVIEW

While a detailed consideration of, arguably, the most important provisions in a commercial lease is beyond the scope of this book, certain core amendments should be sought by a tenant. It is important to establish early on in negotiations with the landlord or the landlord's representative what the purpose of the rent review clause is to be, if there is going to be one in the lease. The landlord will want to ensure that he obtains, at the very least, a return commensurate with market rents at the time the review takes place. On this basis, therefore, it is important, when representing the tenant, to ensure that this is exactly what the rent review clause achieves. The rent review clause is not designed to give the landlord any form of enhanced rental by way of a return over and above that which would be obtainable on a new letting at a market rent. From the tenant's point of view it is important, therefore, to ensure that there is never any question of a '*headline*' rental being obtained and that terms such as 'best' or 'highest' rent are also avoided when determining the open market rent. No doubt the tenant will also wish to avoid an upwards only rent review if he can negotiate this (see **paragraph 4.2.1**). A headline rent is probably best explained using an example. If a tenant agrees to take a lease for five years at a rental of £100,000 pa but he is also granted a twelve-month rent-free period then, while the *headline* rent, ie the rent stated in the lease, remains at £100,000 pa, the *effective* rent payable is actually only £80,000 pa. This concept is vital in understanding the importance of certain disregards and assumptions because if the appropriate provisions are not deleted by the tenant's adviser and the lease is absolutely clear as to what is to be disregarded, ie any rent-free period, an effective rent of £80,000 pa would become an effective rent of £100,000 pa. It is vital therefore that all references to rent-free periods are carefully scrutinised in conjunction with the tenant's surveyor.

> ***Recommendation 6 of the Code: Rent Review:*** *The basis of rent review should generally be to open market rent. Wherever possible, landlords should offer alternatives which are priced on a risk-adjusted basis, including alternatives to upwards only rent reviews; these might include up/down reviews to open market rent with a minimum of the initial rent, or another basis such as annual indexation. Those funding property should make every effort to avoid imposing restrictions on the type of rent review that landlords, developers and/or investors may offer.*

> ***Recommendation 13 of the Code: Rent review negotiation:*** *Landlords and tenants should ensure that they understand the basis upon which rent may be reviewed and the procedure to be followed, including the existence of any strict time limits which could create pitfalls. They should obtain professional advice on these matters well before the review date and also immediately upon receiving (and before responding to) any notice or correspondence on the matter from the other party or his/her agent.*

1.2.1   the assumption that no work has been carried out on the Premises during the Term by the Tenant, his subtenants or their predecessors in title that has diminished the rental value of the Premises <u>other than work carried out in compliance with clause 3.7 STATUTORY OBLIGATIONS</u>

1.2.2   the assumption that if the Premises have been destroyed or damaged they have been fully rebuilt or reinstated <u>unless the failure to reinstate the Premises is due to any act or omission on behalf of the Landlord or the destruction or damage is caused by an Insured Risk [Terrorism whether an Insured Risk or not] or [an Uninsured Risk]</u>

1.2.3   the assumption that the covenants contained in this Lease on the part of <s>the Landlord and</s> the Tenant have been fully performed and observed

1.2.4   the assumption that the Premises are available to let by a willing landlord to a willing tenant in the open market <u>[by one lease] [in whole or in parts]</u> ('the Hypothetical Lease') without a premium being paid by either party and with vacant possession

1.2.5   the assumption that the Premises have already been fitted out and equipped by and at the expense of the incoming tenant so that they are capable of being used by the incoming tenant from the beginning of the Hypothetical Lease for all purposes required by the incoming tenant that would be permitted under this Lease

1.2.1 The words beginning '… other than …' to the end of the paragraph should be included if they are not already there to ensure the tenant is not penalised by having had to pay for works required by statute which diminish the rental value only to have those works disregarded on review.

1.2.2 The addition here is designed to ensure that, if the premises are in a dilapidated state due to a fault on the part of the landlord and through no fault of the tenant, then any assumption about the hypothetical state of the premises reflects this. This may well result in a discount on the reviewed rent. This assumption should only apply in relation to destruction or damage that the tenant is obliged to repair. The second amendment reflects the exclusion of the tenant's liability to repair in respect of Insured and Uninsured Risks by virtue of the amendments made to **clause 3.4.1** relating to the tenant's repair obligation. It should also be noted that it is 'the Premises' as demised which is the subject of the hypothetical lease and that therefore this will not include rights or easements in supplemental agreements or side letters, for example, a right to use a car park or a fire escape.

1.2.3 Landlords will often attempt to insert an assumption that their own covenants have been complied with. This is manifestly unfair on the tenant who may not be enjoying the full benefit of the premises due to some default on the part of the landlord. An assumption, therefore, that the landlord's covenants have been complied with should be resisted and the deletion achieves this. A landlord will argue that if at the date of review he is in breach he should not be saddled with a reduced rent until the next review date or the end of the term if that breach is soon to be remedied. Tenants should, in the face of that argument, argue that there should be a provision whereby the arbitrator (or expert) fixing the reviewed rent in the absence of agreement is directed to establish two levels of rental; the first to subsist for so long as the breach itself subsists and the second to kick in once the breach complained of has been rectified.

1.2.4 The words 'by one lease' should be inserted by the tenant if he is prohibited from subletting part. It follows that if the lease has the assumption that the premises are available to let 'in whole or in parts' the tenant should make an amendment to refer to 'one lease'. This is another example of ensuring that the assumptions reflect reality.

1.2.5 While the intention of this assumption is that the tenant should not be able to claim on rent review a rent-free period for fitting out which has already been done, the landlord has put forward an argument that this assumption means that the hypothetical tenant should pay more than the market rent for the shell if the premises have already been fitted out at no cost to him. One possible solution to overcome this argument is to incorporate an assumption that 'rent concessions for fitting out the premises have already been received by the incoming tenant prior to the beginning of the

1.2.6   the assumption that the Hypothetical Lease contains the same terms as this Lease [including][excluding] the break clause in favour of the Tenant until this has lapsed such break clause to be exercisable at the expiry of the year of the term of the hypo-thetical lease) and except the amount of the Initial Rent and any rent-free period allowed to the Tenant for fitting out the Premises for his occupation and use at the commencement of the Term, but including the provisions for rent review on the Review Dates and except as set out in subparagraph 4 – 1.3.7

1.2.7   the assumption that the term of the Hypothetical Lease is equal in length to the residue unexpired of the Contractual Term [or ten years whichever is the greater] and that such term begins on the relevant review date, that the rent commences to be payable on that date, and that the years during which the tenant covenants to decorate the Premises are at the same intervals after the beginning of the term of the Hypothetical Lease as those specified in this Lease

1.3.8   the assumption that the Hypothetical Lease will be renewed at the expiry of its term under the provisions of the 1954 Act and

Hypothetical Lease'. This reflects reality: the landlord gains no benefit from the fitting out works of the tenant and the tenant gains no discount from the fitting out works which he does not require.

1.2.6 This clause is self-explanatory and the amendment simply seeks to avoid any confusion over the existence or otherwise of any contractual break clause in the actual lease and its interrelation with the hypothetical lease. The option is expressed to be personal to the tenant. It will lapse on the first assignment of the lease and it will not carry over into the hypothetical lease in the absence of express words to provide for this. The tenant may also, for example, have a right to break a lease granted for a term of ten years at the end of the second year of the term so that by the time that the rent review takes effect at the end of the fifth year it will have lapsed. The tenant should only agree to a break clause being included in the hypothetical lease if it has not lapsed since otherwise he is likely to pay a higher rent because the hypothetical lease will be assumed to contain the break clause. Hence the amendment to deal with this point. The likely impact on rent of its existence or otherwise in the hypothetical lease should be discussed with the tenant's surveyor. The author's enquiries have indicated that a possible increase of up to 10% in the rent could result from the existence of a break clause!

1.2.7 Reverting back to the argument set out above at the introduction to Schedule 4, it is important to try and draft the rent review clause to correspond as closely as possible to what actually exists, so that the contractual term of the hypothetical lease is equal to the unexpired residue of the contractual term at the actual date of review. If this has a depressing effect on rental values then so be it. An assumption on any other basis, ie for a term in excess of that which is, in fact, left departs from reality, is wholly artificial and, the author contends, unsustainable. In the absence of any direction to the contrary the term of the hypothetical lease will be the residue unexpired of the contractual term initially granted as at the relevant date but this can be rebutted (see *Canary Wharf Investments v Telegraph Group* [2003] EWHC 1575). While the valuation advice can be taken on what is the most desirable term in the market, this is likely to vary during the term and is not therefore predictable at the time of drafting the rent review provisions. Another possibility is that the term on rent review is that which was originally granted by the lease (see the *Canary Wharf Investments* case referred to above). The frequent compromise is that the term on rent review is the unexpired contractual terms or ten years, whichever is the greater.

1.2.8 If there is a possibility that the *hypothetical lease* will be renewed then this is something that the independent third party determining the rent will take into account when determining the review and be likely to result in a higher rent. He should not be directed to make such an assumption where the lease might be contracted out of the security of tenure provisions of the Landlord and Tenant Act 1954 nor where it is known at the rent review date that the landlord is likely to have grounds for successfully opposing the grant of a new lease

1.3.9   ~~the assumption that every prospective willing landlord and willing tenant is able to recover VAT in full~~

1.3   *'The Disregards'*

'The Disregards' means:

1.3.1   disregard of any effect on rent of the fact that the Tenant, <u>his subtenants, or their predecessors in title or any lawful occupier</u> ~~has~~ <u>have</u> been in occupation of the Premises

1.3.2   disregard of any goodwill attached to the Premises because the business of the Tenant, <u>his subtenants, or their predecessors in title in their respective businesses</u> is or was carried on there and

1.3.3   disregard of any increase in rental value of the Premises attributable at the relevant review date to any improvement to the Premises carried out, ~~with consent where required~~, <u>during the Term or during any period of occupation prior thereto arising out of any agreement to grant the Term or any earlier lease</u> otherwise than in pursuance of an obligation <u>except an obligation contained in clause 3.7 STATUTORY OBLIGATIONS (including, however, for the avoidance of doubt any work undertaken to comply with Part III of the Disability Discrimination Act 1995)</u> to the Landlord or his predecessors in title **or alternatively** <u>[otherwise than by or at the expense of the landlord]</u> either:

on the expiry of the term. If the lease is not contracted out the deletion of this paragraph means that the independent third party is entitled to take account of the possibility (but not the certainty) of the lease being renewed under the Landlord & Tenant Act 1954.

1.2.9   This is a wholly false assumption and may well not in fact be the case. If it is the case then, as referred to above in **paragraph 1.2.8**, the arbitrator/expert will no doubt take account of it. If it is not then the review should reflect reality without false and distorting assumptions being introduced. The tenant should be on the lookout for any other assumptions that depart from reality and normal valuation practice and strenuously resist these (see *Begus Nominees Limited v Deco Limited* [2003] 43 EG 158 and *Dukeminster v Summerfield Properties Co Ltd* [1997] 2 EGLR 125).

1.3.1 and 1.3.2 These amendments are self-explanatory.

1.3.3   The deletion of the words 'with the consent where required' meets the situation where an improvement may not have been formally authorised, eg where there was a *need* to carry out works and formal consent could not be obtained in time and that 'breach' was subsequently waived. The amendment will ensure that if works were, in fact, improvements then those works are not '*rentalised*' which means the reviewed rent will be uplifted to take account of that improvement. If the tenant has actually funded the improvement he will not thank his advisers if his rent is then subsequently enhanced by virtue of it.

The exception referred to in the latter half of this paragraph deals with a situation where the tenant has an obligation, pursuant to statute, to carry out certain works to the premises at its own cost and expense. Here the intention, at least on the landlord's part, is that such works will be rentalised. A particular concern to a tenant here is the likely impact of the Disability Discrimination Act 1995 which will require facilitation works to be carried out to the premises (usually by the tenant) to ensure that there is no discrimination against access for disabled people on account of the physical state of the building. Clearly, there could be huge potential expense here for the tenant, and the proposed amendment makes it clear for the existence of doubt that where the tenant has funded the cost of such facilitation works which have, in turn, enhanced the rental value of the property, then those works are not rentalised and are to be disregarded on review. It is also very important to include the extension of the disregard to improvements made not only during the term but also any earlier occupation, whether under an agreement for lease or any earlier lease. If this is not done on a lease renewal the improvements carried out under the earlier lease will become part of the demised premises under the new lease and the rent payable will not disregard these improvements (see *Brett v Brett Essex Golf Club Limited* [1986] 1 EGLR and *Panther Shop Investments Limited v Keith Popple Limited* [1987] 1 EGLR 131. Further, without the insertion of the words 'accept an obligation'

1.3.3.1   by the Tenant, his subtenants, or their predecessors in title or
            any lawful occupier during the Term or during any period of
            occupation before the Term or

1.3.3.2   by any tenant or subtenant of the Premises or any lawful occu-
            piers before the commencement of the Term provided that the
            Landlord or his predecessors in title have not since the
            improvement was carried out had vacant possession of the
            relevant part of the Premises and

1.3.4   any fixture that the Tenant is entitled to remove at the end of
            the Term

1.3.5   the occupation by the Tenant of the [adjoining] [neighbouring]
            premises known as [   ]

1.3.3.3   ~~disregard of the taxable status of the Landlord or the Tenant
            for the purpose of VAT~~

1.4   'The President'

1.4.1   'The President' means the President for the time being of the
            Royal Institution of Chartered Surveyors or any person autho-
            rised by him to make appointments on his behalf

1.5   'A review period'

1.5.1   References to 'a review period' are references to the period
            beginning on any review date and ending on the day before
            the next review date or in relation to the final review period
            the period beginning on the final review date and ending on
            the last day of the Contractual Term

2   ASCERTAINING THE RENT

2.1   The Rent

           Until the First Review Date the Rent is to be the Initial Rent,
           and thereafter during each successive review period the Rent
           is to be a sum equal to ~~the greater of the rent payable under
           this Lease immediately before the relevant review date, or, if
           payment of rent has been suspended as provided for in this~~

contained in **clause 3.7** 'Statutory obligations' the tenant would effectively pay twice over and the landlord would receive a double benefit (see *Forte & Co Limited v General Accident Life Assurance Limited* [1986] 279 EG 1227. The author's suggestion is that a fair solution is for all improvements to be disregarded other than those made at the expense of the landlord, and this alternative amendment is shown in the text.

1.3.3.1   The tenant should ensure that the disregards are drawn so as to include subtenants or their predecessors in title or any lawful occupier, hence the amendment to **paragraphs 1.3.1, 1.3.2, 1.3.3.1** and **1.3.3.2**.

1.3.3.3   The same arguments apply here as those referred to in **paragraphs 1.2.8** and **1.2.9** above. The review should take account of the actual status of the parties and not be based on assumptions that distort reality and, therefore, distort the open market rent that the tenant should, in fact, be paying.

1.5.1   As was seen in the amendment proposed to **paragraph 1.2.7**, the tenant would be ill-advised to allow a situation to arise whereby he faces a penultimate day rent review. The amendment at the end of this paragraph should be incorporated for the sake of consistency with the earlier amendment.

2.1   The deletion ensures that any rent review which takes place is not an upwards only rent review. At every rent review date the rent will therefore reflect a true open-market rent and again will not be distorted if rental values have fallen since the last rent review date. If the agreed heads of terms make it quite clear that any rent reviews are to be upwards only, it is vital to ensure that a tenant fully understands exactly what that means, ie the rent will *never* fall below the

~~Lease, the rent that would have been payable had there been~~ ~~no such suspension, or~~ the revised rent ascertained in accordance with this schedule

2.2   *Agreement of the Rent*

Six months before each review date, time not being of the essence of the contract, the Landlord and the Tenant must ~~explore the possibility of reaching~~ use reasonable endeavours to reach a written agreement as to the Rent for the following review period and the Rent for that period may be agreed at any time or, in the absence of agreement, is to be determined by an arbitrator not earlier than the relevant review date

2.3   *Open market rent*

The sum to be determined by an arbitrator must be the ~~best~~ sum at which he decides the Premises might reasonably be expected to be let in the open market at the relevant review date making the Assumptions but disregarding the Disregards

2.4   *Conduct of the arbitration*

The arbitration must be conducted in accordance with the Arbitration Act 1996, except that if the arbitrator dies or declines to act the President may, on the application of either the Landlord or the Tenant, appoint another in his place

2.5   *Memoranda of agreement*

Whenever the Rent has been ascertained in accordance with this schedule, memoranda to that effect must be signed by or on behalf of the Landlord and the Tenant and annexed to this document and its counterpart, and ~~the Tenant must pay both~~ ~~parties~~ each party is to pay its own costs in this respect

2.6   *Reimbursement of costs*

If, on publication of the arbitrator's award, the Landlord or the Tenant pays all his fees and expenses, the paying party may, in default of payment within 21 days of a demand to that effect, recover such proportion of them, if any, as the arbitrator awards against the other in the case of the Landlord as rent arrears or in the case of the Tenant by deduction from the Rent

initial rent agreed at the start of the lease even if rental values fall drastically. The author contends that upwards only rent reviews are essentially unsustainable and if a landlord will not accept an upwards and downwards review (sometimes called an 'open market' review), a tenant's adviser should be arguing for a shorter term. In response a landlord may well argue that the tenant should have to pay a higher rent at the commencement of the term to reflect the risk to the landlord that the rent may go down as well as up.

2.2   With respect, the author is not quite sure what the phrase '...*explore the possibility of reaching...*' means or is intended to achieve. The amendment uses words with which lawyers are familiar and which have been interpreted by the courts (see **clause 5.6.3.1**). Wording such as that used in this paragraph also avoids any '*time of the essence*' problems. '*Time of the essence*' issues could fill a chapter or book of their own, but reference to the recent case of *Starmark Enterprises Ltd v CPL Distribution Ltd* [2000] EWCA Civ 1252, [2001] 32 EG 89 is worth noting as it makes clear that 'deeming' properties in the machinery for instigating a rent review can now make time of the essence and thus oblige a tenant to do something about any trigger notice served by the landlord setting out what it believes the reviewed rent should be.

2.3   If there is no other amendment that the tenant can negotiate in the whole lease, this is the one he must stick out for. Inclusion of the word '*best*' means that if, when determining the rent, the expert or arbitrator considers that a range of possible awards is available to him, then, because of the use of the word '*best*' his award will be pitched at the highest figure and indeed any bid from a special bidder, eg a neighbour, will be taken into account. Unless there is a sustainable argument from the landlord (ie that the offices do represent the best offices available in the relevant market) then there is absolutely no reason why the word '*best*' should be included in the definition. The precedent here appoints the independent third party to act as an *arbitrator* here and not as an *expert*. While a detailed study of the differences is beyond the scope of this book, briefly, an expert is likely to be cheaper and quicker and usually less formal. An arbitrator has a statutory framework within which he must operate and has far greater powers. Indeed many see an arbitrator's view as a quasi-judicial one.

2.5   There is no reason and, in the author's view, no sustainable argument why the tenant should pay the costs of the landlord for recording the result of either an agreed or a disputed award.

2.6   Refer to the notes to **clauses 2.1.1** and **3.1.1** to appreciate the significance of the amendment which has been made.

3   PAYMENT OF THE RENT AS ASCERTAINED

3.1   *Where the Rent is not ascertained by a review date*

If the Rent payable during any review period has not been ascertained by the relevant review date, then rent is to continue to be payable at the rate previously payable, such payments being on account of the Rent for that review period

3.2   *Where a review date is not a quarter day*

If the Rent for any review period is ascertained on or before the relevant review date but that date is not a quarter day, then the Tenant must pay to the Landlord ~~on that review date~~ as soon as reasonably practicable after demand the difference between the Rent due for that quarter and the Rent already paid for it.

3.3   *Back-payment where review delayed*

If the Rent payable during any review period has not been ascertained by the relevant review date, then the Tenant must pay to the Landlord ~~on~~ as soon as reasonably practicable after the date on which the Rent is agreed or the arbitrator's award is received by him, any shortfall between the Rent that would have been paid for that period had it been ascertained on or before the relevant review date and the payments made by the Tenant on account and any VAT payable thereon [and interest at the ~~Default Interest Rate~~ Interest Rate ~~in respect of each instalment of rent due on or after that review date on the amount by which the instalment of the Rent that would have been paid had it been ascertained exceeds the amount paid by the Tenant on account, the interest to be payable for the period from the date on which the instalment was due up to the date of payment of the shortfall~~]

3.4   *Effect of counter-inflation provisions*

If at any review date a statute prevents, restricts or modifies the Landlord's right either to review the Rent in accordance with this Lease or to recover any increase in the Rent, then the Landlord may, when the restriction or modification is removed, relaxed or varied during the Contractual Term without prejudice to his rights, if any, to recover any rent the payment of which has only been deferred by statute – on giving not less than 1 ~~week~~ month nor more than 3 ~~week~~ months' notice to the Tenant at any time within 6 months of the restriction or modification being removed, relaxed or varied or within one year of the next Review Date (whichever event is the earlier), time being of the essence, require the Tenant to proceed with any review of the Rent that has been prevented or to review the Rent further where the Landlord's right was

3.2   This amendment gives the tenant a period of grace within which to pay any uplift in the rental. It may be that a substantial hike could cause real cash flow difficulties for the tenant if the shortfall fell to be payable immediately. The landlord has the ultimate sanction of suing the tenant to enforce the award.

3.3   The first amendment seeks to achieve the same effect as that referred to in **paragraph 3.2** above. The subsequent deletion deprives the landlord of any incentive to delay resolution of the review so that any shortfall is subject to an interest payment for the longest possible period and giving a possibly unfair return to the landlord by charging 'the Default Interest Rate' as defined in **clause 1.10**. This rate is a penal rate and the clause should be amended so that the interest is only payable at 'the Interest Rate' as defined in **clause 1.20**.

3.4   The first amendment ensures that there can be no retrospective ground arguable to the landlord once the contractual term of the lease has ended to pursue the tenant for rent. The second and third amendments provide for the tenant being given reasonable time within which to gear up for the impending review. The last amendment prevents the landlord having the right to exercise the review during the residue of the term by putting a time limit on the exercise of the review (since time is not of the essence of the rent review under general principles), and also, it is suggested, provides that the right may not be exercised within one year of the next rent review date to prevent two reviews taking place less than a year apart.

restricted or modified. The date of expiry of the notice is to be treated as a review date – provided that nothing in this paragraph is to be construed as varying any subsequent review date. The Landlord may recover any increase in the Rent with effect from the earliest date permitted by law

SCHEDULE 5 – THE OFFICE COVENANTS

1   USE

1.1   *Use as offices*

The Tenant must not use the Premises for any purpose other than as offices [connected with its business of [ ]]

SCHEDULE 5 – THE OFFICE COVENANTS

1.1   The proposed amendment is drafted so that consideration should be given as to whether the permitted user is as narrowly defined as possible while consistent with the tenant's current proposals and his projected plans for his business. The primary reason for this is to ensure that, at review, the narrowly defined use has the greatest possible effect in reducing or keeping down the rental value. This is unlikely to prove to be acceptable to the landlord but should nonetheless be considered by the tenant. It is not advisable to restrict the use of the premises to a named tenant eg ['Knight & Sons']. From a tenant's point of view this may effectively prevent alienation. From the landlord's point of view this will not give him the control he desires, particularly in the case of a retailer who changes his business and it will also depress the rental value at review and on renewal because it prevents alienation. See *Plinth Property Investments Limited v Mott Hay & Anderson* [1978] 248 EG 1167 where a discount of 31.5% was given to reflect the virtual inalienability of the lease which had a restriction that the offices could only be used for the tenant's business of consulting engineers. Nor is it advisable for a landlord to restrict use to 'the tenant's business' as this may permit whatever business is currently being carried on by whoever is then the tenant and also lead on rent review to an assumption that there is no restriction on the use of the premises. Bad news on both counts for a landlord!

From a practical point of view it is important to ensure that whilst having the permitted user as narrowly defined as possible is ideal for the purpose of the rent review, the user clause must be wide enough to ensure the tenant can expand his business as he chooses and wide enough to ensure that should the tenant ever wish to dispose of the lease it is as marketable as possible. Too narrow a clause may mean the tenant could only dispose of the lease to a competitor. The circumstances of each particular letting may dictate where the greatest emphasis lies. If the permitted use for the premises has been defined by reference to the Use Classes Order complications can arise with its interpretation as a result of **clause 1.51.7**. The author would suggest that if the permitted use is defined by reference to the Use Classes Order 1987 then the following words be added, '...*in relation to which the provisions of clause 1.51.7 shall not apply ...*'.

Recommendation 10 of the Code: Alterations and changes of use: *Landlord's control over alterations and changes of use should not be more restrictive than is necessary to protect the value of the premises and any adjoining or neighbouring premises of the landlord. At the end of the lease the tenant should not be required to remove and make good permitted alterations unless this is reasonably required.*

1.2   *Permitted hours*

Without prior notification to the Landlord [and providing such security arrangements for the protection of the Building as the Landlord reasonably requires] ~~T~~the Tenant must not use and occupy the Premises ~~during~~ outside the Permitted Hours ~~only~~

1.3   *Cesser of business*

The Tenant must not cease carrying on business in the Premises or leave the Premises continuously unoccupied for more than 1 month without notifying the Landlord of his intention so to do [and providing such caretaking and security arrangements for the protection of the Building as the Landlord reasonably requires and the insurers and underwriters require]

1.4   *Noxious discharges*

The Tenant must not knowingly discharge into any of the Conduits or the Adjoining Conduits any oil, grease or other deleterious matter, or any substance that ~~might~~ is likely to be or become a source of danger or injury to the drainage system

1.2   The purpose of this amendment is simply to ensure that, if the tenant requires it, 24-hour access to the property is available. There are not many businesses nowadays which can restrict themselves to working only during certain defined hours. If **clause 1.33** 'Permitted hours' has been successfully deleted this paragraph can be deleted in its entirety. In addition, if the premises are retail premises, account must be taken of the Sunday Trading Act 1994. In certain cases the tenant may have to concede to a landlord an obligation to provide security arrangements, as illustrated by the words which have been added in square brackets.

1.3   There may be good commercial or operational reasons why the premises are to be vacated, eg following a corporate restructuring it may be that the functions previously performed at these offices have been relocated and they have no further use. An absolute obligation to remain in occupation in the premises might well be against the strategic aims of the tenant who might have to live with a long period of vacancy should the lease be difficult to assign. The addition of the word 'continuous' as a tenant's amendment is self-explanatory. The problems that tenants of retail premises have run into over '*keep open*' covenants should be a warning to all tenants of the danger of the landlord bringing a claim for damages for breach of this provision. The additional words provide a possible compromise for a tenant as in **paragraph 1.2** of this schedule.

Whilst not really relevant in the context of a lease of office space, the author feels that mention needs to be made of the possibility of the landlord attempting to insert a *keep open covenant*. The author acts for a number of retail operators who object to such a clause because, quite rightly in the author's view, they feel that whether they keep a shop open or not is really a commercial decision for them and, provided the rent and other obligations in the lease are complied with, is really nothing to do with the landlord. The courts, too, have also tended to refuse to interfere in terms of granting mandatory injunctions requiring the premises to be kept open. This was typified by the House of Lords in their judgment in *Co-operative Insurance Society Ltd v Argyll Stores Holdings Ltd* [1997] 23 EG 141. However, the tenant's advisers would be ill advised to rely on this entirely, because if a landlord is able to show that closure of premises has resulted in a loss to it, it is entitled to make a claim for substantive losses. A typical example would be the closure of a store by an anchor tenant. All in all, from a tenant's point of view, keep open covenants should be resisted and therefore deleted in the negotiating process. From a landlord's point of view the onerous nature of the covenant would undoubtedly have an adverse effect on the rent payable on review.

1.4   The first amendment imparts knowledge to negate strict liability (see **clause 3.15.1**) and the second imposes a greater burden of proof.

1.5   *Window cleaning*

The Tenant must clean both sides of all windows and window frames in the Premises ~~at least once every month~~ as often as occasion shall reasonably require

1.6   *Sound audible outside*

The Tenant must not play or use in the Premises any musical instrument, audio or other equipment or apparatus that produces sound that may be heard outside the Premises [if the Landlord ~~in his absolute~~ discretion reasonably considers such sounds to be ~~undesirable~~ amount to a legal nuisance and gives notice to the tenant to that effect]

1.7   *Ceiling and floor loading*

1.7.1   Heavy items

The Tenant must not bring onto or permit to remain on the Premises any safes, machinery, goods or other articles that will ~~or may~~ strain or damage the Premises or any part of them

1.7.2   Protection of ceilings

The Tenant must not without the consent of the Landlord (such consent not to be unreasonably withheld or delayed) suspend anything from any ceiling on the Premises

1.8   *Expert advice*

If the Tenant applies for the Landlord's consent under paragraph 1.7.2 the Landlord may consult any engineer or other person in relation to the ceiling loading proposed by the Tenant, and the Tenant must repay the reasonable and proper fees of the engineer or other person to the Landlord as soon as reasonably practicable following ~~on~~ demand

2   COMMON PARTS

2.1   *Care of the Common Parts*

The Tenant must not cause the Common Parts or any other land, roads or pavements adjoining the Building and belonging to the Landlord to become untidy or dirty

2.2   Display of goods outside

The Tenant must not display or deposit anything whatsoever outside the Premises for display or sale or for any other purpose, or save in emergency cause any obstruction of the Common Parts

1.5   While the amendment speaks for itself, it is important to bear in mind the wider implications of very strictly drawn clauses and the interrelationship they have with other clauses in the lease, eg a tenant's break clause which is conditional upon *strict compliance* with covenants elsewhere (see **clause 8.16**). In the light of the interpretation placed by the court on such strict preconditions even an immaterial breach (such as default in window cleaning) could prove fatal from the tenant's point of view and so result in the loss of a very precious commodity such as a break clause.

1.6   This amendment means that the sound audible outside must amount to a legal nuisance which is consistent with the amendments made to **clause 3.10.1** to which reference should be made.

1.7.1   The clause as originally drafted gives the landlord an arguable case that the tenant's proposals may cause the strain or damage without any form of quantitative assessment. The deletion prevents this happening.

1.7.2   The proposed amendment changes an absolute prohibition into a qualified one and gives the tenant the opportunity to argue that the landlord is acting unreasonably.

1.8   The amendments here are self-explanatory.

2.1   It is unfair that the landlord should seek to police areas outside its own ownership by imposing restrictions on the tenant and the amendment meets this point.

2.2   The amendment here is self-explanatory and would allow the tenant to obstruct the common part in the case of an emergency.

2.3   *Machinery*

2.3.1   Noisy machinery

The Tenant must not <u>without the Landlord's consent (such consent not to be unreasonably withheld or delayed)</u> install or use in or on the Premises any machinery or apparatus <u>other than usual office machinery</u> that will cause noise or vibration that can be heard or felt in nearby premises or outside the Premises or that may cause structural damage

2.3.2   *Maintenance of machinery*

In order to avoid <u>physical</u> damage to the Premises, the Tenant must keep all machinery and equipment on the Premises ('the Machinery') properly maintained and in good working order and for that purpose must employ reputable contractors ~~to be approved by the Landlord whose approval may not be unreasonably refused~~ ('the Contractors') to carry out <u>as often as occasion shall reasonably require</u> ~~regular periodic~~ inspection and maintenance of the Machinery

2.4   *Renewal of parts*

The Tenant must renew all working and other parts of the Machinery as and when <u>reasonably</u> necessary or when recommended by the Contractors

~~2.5~~   *~~Operation~~*

~~The Tenant must ensure by directions to his staff and otherwise that the Machinery is properly operated~~

3   UNLOADING

3.1   *Loading bays to be used*

The Tenant must not load or unload any goods or materials from any vehicle unless the vehicle is parked in the loading bay coloured yellow on ~~the~~ Plan <u>No. 3</u>, and must not cause congestion of that or any adjoining loading bays or <u>unnecessary</u> inconvenience to any other user of it or them

3.2   *Standing vehicles*

The Tenant must not permit any vehicles belonging to him or any persons calling on the Premises expressly or by implication with his authority to stand on the service roads or any pavements or, except when and for so long as they are actually loading or unloading goods and materials, on the loading bays, and must use ~~his best~~ <u>reasonable</u> endeavours to ensure that such persons do not permit any vehicle so to stand

2.3.1   The first amendment provides that every application by the tenant to install machinery or apparatus is considered on its own merits. It may well be that the criteria referred to do, in fact, provide the benchmark against which the landlord will be able to judge whether he has grounds for withholding consent but at least, once again, the amendment inserts the concept of reasonableness and gives the tenant the opportunity of arguing the point.

   The second amendment excluding 'usual office machinery' is self-explanatory.

2.3.2   These are, the author contends, matters which are the personal responsibility of the tenant in running his business and have nothing whatsoever to do with the landlord. The word *reputable* gives the landlord the necessary comfort.

2.4   This amendment is self-explanatory.

2.5   This again is an internal management issue for the tenant and has no relevance to the relationship of landlord and tenant. The clause should be deleted on this basis.

3.1   The first amendment seeks to ensure, once again, consistency in referring to the plans. The second reflects the fact that unloading a vehicle, even in designated parking areas, will inevitably on occasions cause an inconvenience to somebody or other.

3.2   The amendment here is made in consequence of the court's decisions that *best endeavours* is something more onerous than *reasonable endeavours* (see **clause 5.6.3.1**) and, in the context of what is envisaged, an obligation to use best endeavours may involve expenditure of money or the involvement of management time on the tenant's part wholly out of proportion to their ability to control visitors to the premises.

3.3   *Use of goods entrances required*

The Tenant must not convey any goods or materials to or from the Premises except through the entrances and service areas provided for the purpose

4   HEATING, COOLING AND VENTILATION

4.1   *Interference prohibited*

The Tenant must not <u>knowingly </u>do anything that interferes |
with the heating, cooling ventilation or air conditioning of the Common Parts or that imposes an additional load on any heating, cooling ventilation or air conditioning plant and equipment in the Building

4.2   *Operation of equipment*

During the Permitted Hours, the Tenant must operate the ventilation equipment in the Premises which comprise parts of the air conditioning of the Building in accordance with the <u>reasonable written </u>regulations made by the Landlord from time to time for that purpose<u> and served on the Tenant</u> |

5   REGULATIONS

5.1   The Tenant must comply with all <u>reasonable </u>regulations made |
<u>in the interests of good estate management </u>by the Landlord <u>and notified to the Tenant in writing</u> from time to time for the management of the Building <u>PROVIDED ALWAYS that if there shall be any inconsistency between any such regulations and the terms of this lease then the terms of this lease shall prevail</u> |

6   NAMEPLATES OR SIGNS

6.1   Before <u>or as soon as reasonably practicable after </u>occupying |
the Premises for the purpose of his business at the commencement of the Term and following a permitted assignment or subletting, the Tenant must provide the Landlord with details of the information that he wishes to have included in the nameplates or signs referred to in paragraph 2-3 DISPLAY OF NAMEPLATES OR SIGNS, and must pay to the Landlord <u>as soon as reasonably practicable following</u>on demand the <u>reasonable and proper </u>charges of the Landlord for making and |
installing every such nameplate or sign

4.1   The amendment is self-explanatory and once again avoids the harsh consequences of strict liability.

4.2   The first amendment provides that any such regulations which are needed must be both reasonable and have been committed to paper so there is no dispute as to their content. The second amendment prevents the tenant being liable where written regulations may have been made but he has not had notice of these.

5.1   The author's first instinct is to delete this clause in its entirety. The lease has been *freely* negotiated between the parties and therefore *any* provision which seeks to give either party the right to unilaterally alter the basis on which the landlord manages the building or otherwise must be manifestly unfair. However, this is likely to be resisted by a landlord and therefore the first two amendments ensure that any such regulations are reasonable, are made in the interests of good estate management, are notified to the tenant in writing and are not simply introduced to alter, unilaterally, the arrangements for management of the building or otherwise agreed in the lease negotiations. The proviso ensures that any such regulations will not prevail if they are inconsistent with the terms of the lease so, in effect, the landlord can add new regulations but *not* alter existing contractual obligations.

6   Ideally the tenant should seek to strike this clause out in its entirety. If not successful then the tenant should attempt to incorporate those amendments indicated all of which are self-explanatory. To have an *absolute* obligation to provide this information – and indeed to have such an obligation at all – may be contrary to the tenant's policy; for good commercial reasons such as their wish to keep his presence within a particular building a secret for as long as possible.

SCHEDULE 6 – THE SERVICE CHARGE AND SERVICES

1   DEFINITIONS

In this schedule the terms defined below have the meanings given in this paragraph

1.1   *'A financial year'*

References to 'a financial year' are references to the period commencing on 1 January in any year and ending on 31 December in the same year or such other annual period as the Landlord in his <u>reasonable </u>discretion determines as being that for which his accounts~~, either generally or~~ in respect of the Building, are to be made up

1.2   *'The Management Premises'*

'The Management Premises' means all <u>(if any) of </u>the adminis-trative and control offices and storage areas, staff rooms and other areas <u>reasonably and properly </u>maintained by the Landlord for the purpose of managing the Building and per-forming the Landlord's obligations under this Lease ~~together with any living accommodation provided by the Landlord for security guards, caretakers or other staff employed by him for purposes connected with the Building~~

1.3   *'Other lettable premises'*

References to 'other lettable premises' are references to prem-ises in the Building that are let, or are ~~from time to time allo-cated for ~~<u>designed for </u>letting, by the Landlord, other than the Premises, and respectively include and exclude, where appli-cable, the equivalent parts of the Building included in and excluded from the Premises as described in Schedule 1 THE PREMISES

1.4   *'The Plant'*

'The Plant' means all the electrical, mechanical and other plant, machinery, equipment, furnishings, furniture, fixtures and fittings of ornament or utility in use for common benefit from time to time on, in or at the Building, including, without prejudice to the generality of the foregoing, goods and pas-senger lifts, lift shafts, escalators, passenger conveyors, heat-ing, cooling, lighting ventilation and air conditioning equipment, cleaning equipment, internal and public tele-phones, public address systems, fire precaution equipment, fire and burglar alarm systems, closed circuit television, refuse compactors and all other such equipment, including standby and emergency systems

SCHEDULE 6 – THE SERVICE CHARGE AND SERVICES

> *Recommendation 3 of the Code: Financial matters:* Landlords should provide estimates of any service charges and other outgoings in addition to the rent. Parties should be open about their financial standing to each other, on the understanding that information provided will be kept confidential unless already publicly available or there is proper need for disclosure. The terms on which any cash deposit is to be held should be agreed and documented.

> *Recommendation 20 of the Code: Service charges:* Landlords should observe the Guide to Good Practice on Service Charges in Commercial Properties. Tenants should familiarise themselves with that Guide and should take professional advice if they think they are being asked to pay excessive service charges. (Note: the newly produced RICS Guide in relation to service charges referred to in the preamble to this book is, of course, just as relevant here. Called 'Service Charges in Commercial Property', it can be found at www.servicechargecode.co.uk.)

1.1   The first amendment seeks to ensure that the landlord does not manipulate the accounting reference dates each year to his own ends. The second amendment qualifies the otherwise unfettered discretion of the landlord in the operation of his wider accounting procedures.

1.2   The clause, as originally drafted, is far too wide from the tenant's point of view and, the author contends, absolutely unacceptable. If the landlord considers it necessary to provide living accommodation for security guards, caretakers or other staff employed by him for management reasons this is not something which the tenants in the building should actually pay for. To sustain an argument for including the deleted words, the landlord would have to show a very high degree of benefit to the tenant and other occupiers of the building.

1.3   It may appear here that the amendment does not add anything to the wording as originally drafted but the author would contend that this gives a narrower construction and is, therefore, preferable. This definition is important as referred to in **paragraph 2.7** of the Schedule. Refer to the note on this paragraph.

2   SERVICE CHARGE PROVISIONS

2.1   *Certificate of the Landlord's Expenses*

As soon as reasonably practicable after (but in any event within 2 months of the end of) each financial year the Landlord
must ensure that the Accountant issues a certificate addressed
to the Tenant containing a full and accurate summary of the
Landlord's Expenses for that financial year, and a full and
accurate summary of any expenditure that formed part of the
Landlord's Expenses in respect of a previous financial year but
has not been taken into account in the certificate for any previous financial year. ~~A copy of the certificate must be supplied
by the Landlord to the Tenant~~In this Certificate the Accountant
is to acknowledge that he has a duty of care to the Tenant and
the Landlord will permit the Tenant at any time within 3
months of the issue of the certificate to inspect any vouchers
receipts of other relevant information for any items contained
in or referred to in the certificate

2.2   *Omissions from the certificate*

Omission by the Accountant from a certificate of the
Landlord's Expenses of any expenditure incurred in the financial year to which the certificate relates is ~~not~~ to preclude the
inclusion of that expenditure in any subsequent certificate

2.3   ~~Deemed~~ *Landlord's Expenses*

In any financial year the Landlord's Expenses ~~are to be
deemed to~~ shall include:

2.3.1   such fair and reasonable part of all costs and expenditure in
respect of or incidental to all or any of the recurring services
and other matters referred to in paragraph 3 of this Schedule
reasonably and properly, ~~whenever~~ paid or incurred ~~whether
before or~~ during the Term) ~~including reasonable provision for
anticipated expenditure as the Surveyor in his discretion allo-
cates to that financial year~~ and having regard to both the
Contractual Term (as originally granted) and the unexpired
Contractual Term at the date such costs and expenses are paid
or incurred

2.3.2   ~~an amount equal to the fair annual rental value of the
Management Premises, as certified by the Surveyor and if the
Landlord or a person connected with the Landlord or
employed by the Landlord attends to (1) the supervision and
management of the provision of services for the Building,
and/or (2) the preparation of statements or certificates of the
Landlord's Expenses, and/or (3) the auditing of the Landlord's
Expenses, and/or (4) the collection of rents from the Building,
then an expense is to be deemed to be paid or a cost incurred~~

2.1　　　The first amendment imposes a strict time limit within which the landlord's certificate as to the service charge expenditure must be issued to the tenant. In the author's experience many landlords are often guilty of serious delay in providing an accurate or detailed summary of the service charge expenditure but, unfortunately, many tenants are just as bad in chasing them up! The second and third amendments attempt to ensure that the landlord does not give a 'back of the fag packet' summary by putting him under an obligation to prepare a full and accurate summary of the service charge expenditure. The final amendment to this paragraph will leave the accountant in no doubt that he is liable to be sued by the tenant if he is negligent, breaching the duty of care he owes to the tenant. While this will not prove attractive to either the landlord or the accountant, it is certainly something that the tenant should press for. The tenant should argue that it is, after all, *his* money (and that of his co-tenants in the building) which the summary and the certificate relate to.

2.2　　　This amendment provides that if through bad or inadequate accounting or management practices an item of expenditure is overlooked in any year there is no reason why subsequently the tenant should be liable to pay for this oversight. While this argument is not likely to find favour with the landlord because he will argue that the services have been provided to the benefit of the tenant, it will ensure accurate accountability on a year-on-year basis.

2.3.1　　The first amendment, once again, will ensure that all the recovery of expenditure under the service charge is dealt with on a year-on-year basis. There is no reason why a current tenant in occupation should subsidise a former tenant by contributing to an item of service charge expenditure incurred before he himself took up occupation and from which he derived no benefit. Taking the line of the landlord's drafting to the extreme, this would mean that all items of capital expenditure incurred in relation to provision of services could be recharged to the tenants subsequently rather than, as they clearly should do, form part of the landlord or developer's development or initial fit out costs; this, clearly, is unreasonable and unacceptable from the tenant's point of view. The final deletion relating to '*anticipated expenditure*' may be more difficult to sustain but inclusion of the word '*reasonable*' to qualify the anticipated expenditure may prove to be an acceptable compromise.

There is now some case law to back up the tenant's argument that there should be some fetter on the landlord's ability to recover costs it incurs. The case of *Scottish Mutual Assurance plc v Jardine Public Relations Ltd* [1999] EGCS 43 held that a tenant under a three-year lease was not liable to contribute towards roof repairs which were considered to be non-urgent that were felt much more appropriate to a longer-term letting. In addition, the standard to which works should be carried out by a landlord for which the tenant had to pay is influenced by the length of the lease term (see *Fluor Daniel Properties Ltd v Shortlands Investment Ltd* [2001] 2 EGLR 103).

~~by the Landlord, being a fee not exceeding that which inde-~~
~~pendent agents might properly have charged for the same~~
~~work~~

2.3.2   There shall be excluded from the Landlord's Expenses in any
financial year any costs and expenditure paid or incurred
which is attributable to:

(a)   damage or otherwise by an Insured Risk [Terrorism
whether Insured Risk or not] **or alternatively** [an
Uninsured Risk]

(b)   the initial capital cost of the construction of the Building
or Premises

(c)   remedying of an Inherent Defect in the Building Plant or
the Premises

(d)   the improvement of any part of the Building Plant or the
Premises

(e)   any liability or expense for which other tenants or occupiers of the Building will individually be responsible
under the terms of their tenancies or other arrangements
by which they use or occupy the Building

(f)   special concessions given by the Landlord to any other
tenant or occupier of the Building

(g)   obligation to comply with any statutory requirements
including without prejudice the generality of the foregoing environmental statutes regulations and orders

2.4   *Certificates conclusive*

Any certificate of the Landlord's Expenses, and any certificate
of the Surveyor or Accountant in connection with the
Landlord's Expenses, is (save in relation to manifest error or
fraud or mistake of law) to be conclusive as to the matters it
purports to certify

2.5   *Payment*

[Subject to any maximum payment agreed elsewhere in the
Schedule] for each financial year the Tenant must pay the
Service Charge Percentage of the Landlord's Expenses

2.6   **Variation of the Service Charge Percentage**

The Service Charge Percentage may be varied to the extent
that the Surveyor (acting reasonably) considers ~~appropriate~~
fair and proper and in accordance with the principles of good

2.3.2   The author finds this paragraph unacceptable in its entirety. It should be strongly resisted and deleted. It is suggested that this subparagraph should be replaced by a provision that expressly sets out items of expenditure and costs which should be excluded from 'the Landlord's Expenditure' in line with the 'Guide to Good Practice in respect of Service Charges in Commercial Leases' published in August 2000 and also in the new RICS Code 'Service Charges in Commercial property' which comes into effect in April 2007. The Guide specifically provides that service charge costs should not include:

> The initial costs incurred in relation to the original design and construction of the fabric, plant or equipment, ie inherent defects (para 17(a) of the Guide)
>
> Any setting up costs reasonably to be considered as part of the original development costs of the property (para 17(b) of the Guide)
>
> Improvement costs above the cost of normal maintenance, repair or replacement (para 17(c) of the Guide)
>
> Future development costs (para 17(d) of the Guide)
>
> Costs as to matters between the owners and individual occupiers, for instance enforcement of covenants or collection of rent, costs of letting units and alterations and rent reviews (para 17(e) of the Guide)
>
> Cost of any special concession given by the owner to any one occupier (para 60 of the Guide).

2.4   This amendment is self-explanatory and provides the tenant with a peg on which to hang an argument if either of these three eventualities exist. With regard to the additional words 'mistake of law' the House of Lords in *Kleinwort v Lincoln City Council* [1998] 51 EG 76 overruled earlier law and held that payments made under mistake of law could be recovered (see *University's Superannuation v Marks & Spencer* [1999] L&TR 862 for the application of this principle to service charges).

2.5   Refer to **paragraph 2.8** and the note on this in respect of capping the service charge.

2.6   This amendment is self-explanatory and again introduces the concepts of reasonableness and fair and proper and in addition the principles of good estate management by reference to the 'Guide to Good Practice in respect of Service Charges in Commercial Leases'.

estate management contained in the Guide to Good Practice in respect of Service charges in Commercial Leases

2.7   Landlord's contribution

The Landlord is to have no liability to contribute to the Landlord's Expenses except in relation to any other lettable premises for which no contribution is payable by an occupier or other person

2.8   Payment on account

For each financial year the Tenant must pay to the Landlord on account of the Service Charge such a sum as the Surveyor (acting reasonably) certifies to be fair and reasonable having regard to the likely amount of the Service Charge up to a maximum of £[ ] for any one financial year. That sum must be paid in advance, ~~without deduction or set off,~~ by equal instalments on the usual quarter days, the first instalment to be paid on the quarter day immediately before the commencement of the financial year in question and is to be held by the Landlord in a separate nominated account (interest accruing to the amount) until such money is actually expended by the Landlord, the Tenant being given credit for any interest so accruing. If in all the circumstances the Surveyor deems it fair and reasonable to do so then ~~D~~during any financial year he may revise the contribution on account of the Service Charge for that financial year so as to take into account any actual or expected increase in expenditure, and as soon as reasonably practicable after a revision the Surveyor must certify the amount of the revised contribution

2.9   Service charge for the first financial year

The sum payable for the financial year current at the date of this document is to be the Initial Provisional Service Charge, of which the Tenant must, on the date of this document, pay to the Landlord a due proportion calculated from day to day in respect of the period from [the date hereof] or [the Rent Commencement Date] to the next quarter day after the date of this document

2.10   Final account and adjustments

As soon as reasonably practicable (but in any event within 2 months) after the end of each financial year, the Landlord must furnish to the Tenant with an account of the Service Charge payable by him for that financial year, credit being given for payments made by the Tenant on account. ~~Within 7 days of~~As soon as reasonably practicable after the furnishing of such an account, the Tenant must pay the Service Charge, or any balance of it payable, to the Landlord. The Landlord must allow

2.7   This follows a recommendation in the 'Guide to Good Practice in respect of Service Charges in Commercial Leases', paragraph 60, which provides that the service charge costs should not include costs attributable to unlet premises (commonly known as voids) or parts of the building occupied by the landlord or its employees or agents. The definition of 'other lettable premises' is in **paragraph 1.3**.

2.8   What a tenant ideally wants at the outset is, as accurately as possible, an estimate of his total expenditure in respect of the premises for at least the first three or five years of the lease depending on the frequency of the rent review dates. A service charge provision makes such an accurate estimate almost, if not actually, impossible bearing in mind its fluctuating nature. While, no doubt, the tenant will have made enquiries, either prior to the grant of the lease or prior to the assignment, as to whether or not in the foreseeable future any major capital expenditure on the premises is known or anticipated it is not always possible for the landlord to predict them or he may not choose to show his hand. One way to ensure that there is a fixed liability is to *cap* a service charge such that it never exceeds an annual figure either expressed to be a certain amount of expenditure per square foot or a global figure for each year possibly increased annually either by reference to a fixed percentage or by reference to increases in the retail price index. This amendment ensures that this idea is at least considered. Many landlords seek to resist a cap on the basis that they want clean leases and do not want to have to subsidise management expenses from their rental income. Whether this proves to be acceptable is likely to be dependent on the relative bargaining positions of the parties. It is something which should however be considered. The deletion has been fully discussed at **clauses 2.1.1** and **3.1.1** while the additional reference to payment into a separate account is self-explanatory. The final amendment qualifies the ability of the surveyor to review the percentage contribution so that it must be fair and reasonable in all the circumstances for this to happen.

2.10   The first amendment is the same amendment as that made to **paragraph 2.1** of the Schedule with the same arguments applying for its inclusion. The second amendment seeks to ensure that a hefty service charge balance does not place the tenant in cash-flow difficulties, while the final amendment provides for repayment of any credit balance on the service charge account at the end of the term when the tenant vacates. It is the author's experience that in such circumstances landlords may well try to ensure that there is little if any refund due to the tenant and this matter needs to be closely watched by the tenant in questioning the landlord's financial management.

any amount overpaid by the Tenant to him against future payments of Service Charge, whether on account or not. and at
the end of the financial year current at the end of the outstanding Term the Landlord must repay any overpayment forthwith.

3   THE SERVICES

The Services are:

3.1   repairing, maintaining and decorating and, whenever the
Landlord (acting reasonably) in order to repair considers the
Retained Position, incapable of economic repair replacing or
renewing and decorating the Retained Parts

3.2   operating, maintaining, repairing and, whenever the Landlord
(acting reasonably) , considers it appropriate, the Plant incapable of economic repair renewing, replacing or modifying
the Plant

3.3   placing and running maintenance contracts for the Building,

3.4   providing the Plant that the Landlord, (acting reasonably) considers necessary or desirable, or that is required by law or by
any government department or local, public or regulatory or
other authority or court to be supplied and maintained, (but
excluding including the initial capital expenditure) and including expenditure on replacement of any machinery (including
motor vehicles) articles and materials for, for example, refuse
collection and firefighting,

3.5   providing suitable facilities for disposing of refuse, compact-
ing it or removing it from the Building

3.6   supplying hot and cold water to the lavatory facilities in the
Retained Parts during normal business hours, and providing
towels, soap, toilet paper and other appropriate supplies, and
staffing the lavatory facilities

3.7   providing lighting in the Retained Parts

3.8   providing central heating and if appropriate air conditioning to
the Premises and the Common Parts during the Permitted
Hours

3.9   cleaning the windows and other glass of the Retained Parts

3.10   supplying, maintaining, servicing and keeping in good condition and, wherever incapable of economic repair the Landlord
considers it appropriate, renewing and replacing all fixtures,
fittings, furnishings, equipment and any other things the
Landlord may (acting reasonably) considers desirable for per-

Recommendation 7 of the Code: Repairs and services: The tenant's repairing obligations, and any repairs costs included in service charges, should be appropriate to the length of the term and the condition and age of the property at the start of the lease. Where appropriate the landlord should consider appropriately priced alternatives to full repairing terms.

3.1 This is a very comprehensive list and not all the items listed will be appropriate to the particular building concerned. The solicitor acting for the tenant should, in conjunction with the tenant and/or his surveyor, look very critically at the list and delete those items which are not appropriate for any reason. **Paragraph 2.3.2** of this schedule does, however, seek to exclude various items of expenditure that the landlord may incur but should not be able to recover if the 'Guide to Good Practice in Service Charges' is being invoked. The amendment does, however, seek to ensure that the obligation on the landlord to replace an item as part of his repair obligation only applies when the Retained Parts are beyond economic repair.

3.2 The same arguments can be put forward here as in relation to **paragraph 3.1** of the Schedule.

3.4 Again it is necessary to decide whether as a point of principle the service charge is to cover these items. If so, the amendments seek to limit the circumstances in which the provisions would apply so that the landlord is not given a free hand. It is the author's view that the provision of many of the items referred to is a management or investment expense for which the landlord should be responsible and not, therefore, a cost which should be passed on through the service charge and be payable by the tenant.

3.8 Once again, this is a matter of principle. Should the tenant be funding air-conditioning as it will no doubt improve the capital value of the premises? The installation of air-conditioning in the premises and common parts once its initial construction has been completed is likely to prove so troublesome and inconvenient that many tenants will want to resist this.

3.10 Once again the same arguments have to be considered here as in relation to **paragraph 3.1** of the Schedule.

forming the Services or for the appearance or upkeep of the Retained Parts

3.11   carrying out inspections and tests of the Retained Parts, including the Plant, that the Landlord (<u>acting reasonably)</u> from time to time considers necessary or desirable

3.12   planting, tidying, tending and landscaping any appropriate part of the Common Parts in such manner as the Landlord <u>acting reasonably</u> from time to time considers appropriate

3.13   providing, replacing and renewing trees, shrubs, flowers, grass and other plants, flags, decorative lights and other decorations, decorative or drinking fountains or other amenities that the Landlord (<u>acting reasonably)</u> from time to time thinks fit to provide or maintain in the Building, and providing<u>, and</u> maintaining, ~~replacing and renewing~~ seats or benches in the Common Parts

3.14   employing such persons as the Landlord<u>, (acting reasonably)</u> considers necessary or desirable <u>in the interests of good estate management</u> from time to time in connection with providing any of the Services, performing the Landlord's other obligations in this Lease ~~and collecting rents accruing to the Landlord from the Building, with all incidental expenditure including, but without limiting the generality of the above, remuneration, payment of statutory contributions and such other health, pension, welfare, redundancy and similar or ancillary payments and any other payments the Landlord thinks desirable or necessary, and providing work clothing~~

~~3.15~~   ~~discharging any amounts the Landlord may be liable to pay towards the expense of making, repairing, maintaining, rebuilding and cleaning anything — for example ways, roads, pavements, sewers, drains, pipes, watercourses, party walls, party structures, party fences and other conveniences — that are appurtenant to the Building or are used for the Building in common with any adjoining property of the Landlord~~

3.16   erecting, providing, maintaining, <u>and when incapable of economic repair</u> renewing and replacing noticeboards, notices and other signs in the Building as the Landlord, (<u>acting reasonably),</u> from time to time considers appropriate

~~3.17~~   ~~administering and managing the Building, performing the Services, performing the Landlord's other obligations in this Lease and preparing statements or certificates of and auditing the Landlord's Expenses,~~

3.11   This amendment is self-explanatory.

3.12   This amendment is self-explanatory.

3.13   The first amendment is self-explanatory while the second is based on the *replacing and renewing* argument referred to in **paragraph 3.1** of the Schedule. It is the author's view that replacing and renewing seats or benches in the common parts goes beyond what is envisaged by traditional service charge provisions and should be deleted. If not, where will it all end? What benefit does this bring to the tenant? This example does highlight the need for the tenant to consider carefully each element of all the service charge provisions on their own merits and question their appropriateness in relation to the premises and building to which the provisions relate.

3.14   The first two amendments are self-explanatory. To charge a tenant for collecting the rents which he has to pay is surely rubbing salt into his wounds and should be resisted. The other items deleted in this clause are, once again, items so far removed from providing services for the tenant in his enjoyment of the premises that they themselves again ought to be deleted.

3.15   An obligation to contribute towards the items referred to in this clause as originally drawn is no doubt a matter the landlord will have taken on board in deciding whether or not to purchase the freehold or the head leasehold interest in the building. These are matters which relate to the freehold and not to the tenant's occupation of the premises. If there is a potential liability on the part of the landlord here then this should have been taken into account in the rental negotiations.

3.16   The first amendment is based on the same arguments as are referred to in **paragraph 3.1** of the Schedule. The second amendment provides that the concept of reasonableness on the part of the landlord is introduced in deciding whether or not it needs to undertake such matters.

3.17   This clause as originally drawn again rubs salt into the tenant's wounds. If the landlord wishes to farm out management of the building then this is a *pure* management cost which he himself should absorb. This argument is unlikely to find much favour with the landlord who will almost certainly want to pass on such costs to all the tenants of the building. If the clause cannot be negotiated out then at least some fetter on what the landlord can charge should be inserted, eg a *reasonable and proper* sum or an agreed fixed sum or a percentage of the overall service charge.

3.18   providing and performing all services of any kind whatsoever that the Landlord, (acting reasonably) and in the interests of good estate management and for the benefit of the tenants in the Building, from time to time provides

3.19   discharging all existing or future taxes, rates, charges, duties, assessments, impositions and outgoings whatsoever in respect of the Retained Parts, including, without prejudice to the generality of the above, those for water, electricity, gas and telecommunications

3.20   policing the Building, controlling traffic and pedestrians and providing such security staff as the Landlord (acting reasonably) from time to time thinks fit and proper, and providing, maintaining, replacing and renewing security equipment in the Building

3.21   paying any interest on any loan or overdraft raised for the purpose of defraying the Landlord's Expenses

3.22   taking any steps the Landlord, acting reasonably, from time to time considers appropriate for complying with, making representations against, or otherwise contesting or dealing with any statutory or other obligation affecting or alleged to affect the Building, including any notice, regulation or order of any government department, local, public, regulatory or other authority or court, compliance with which is not the direct liability of the Tenant or any Tenant of any part of the Building

3.23   subject to **clause 4.2.3** discharging the cost of any service or matter the Landlord (acting reasonably) thinks proper for the better and more efficient management and use of the Building and the comfort and convenience of its occupants will improve the amenities in the Building for the benefit of the Tenant and the other tenants in the Building or enable the management of the Building to be more efficiently conducted

3.24   renting any item used for carrying out any of the matters referred to in this schedule

3.25   abating any legal nuisance affecting the Building, except to the extent that abating it is the liability of any tenant of the Building and

3.26   keeping appropriate areas of the Common Parts open for servicing the Premises and other units in the Building from time to time

3.18   If additional services other than those specifically set out are to be provided by virtue of this *sweeper clause* there must be some benefit in it for the tenant or the majority of the tenants in the building. The landlord should not be able to implement a scheme within the building to make unlet premises more attractive for the purpose of securing a new letting.

3.20   The first amendment is self-explanatory and the second amendment reflects the principle discussed at **paragraph 3.1** above.

3.21   If the landlord cannot fund items of expenditure such as these then it is completely iniquitous that the tenant should pay the interest costs incurred on money borrowed to provide them. This clause is absolutely unacceptable from a tenant's point of view and should be deleted.

3.22   The same arguments which were put forward in relation to **paragraph 3.15** apply here also. These are *pure* management issues which may well involve substantial expenditure and in the author's view are matters for which the landlord should be responsible.

3.23   The landlord will seek as comprehensive a list of services as possible and often, as in this case, include a sweeping-up clause to cover unforeseen items of expenditure and to allow services to be varied, added to or extended. The tenant should resist too wide a clause on the basis that this operates as a blank cheque and certainly qualify this so that any additional or extended service has to improve the amenities in the building for the benefit of the tenant or enable the management of the building to be more efficiently conducted.

3.24   Inclusion of this clause effectively means that the tenant will end up funding the initial costs incurred by the landlord. This again is unacceptable for the reasons set out in **paragraph 3.15**.

3.25   This amendment ensures that the nuisance has to give rise to a tortious claim in damages and is more than what in every day language amounts to a nuisance in the sense of being an annoyance or interference to a third party. The proviso at the end of the Schedule seeks simply to expand on the principle referred to in **paragraph 2.3.2** whereby if third party money is (or should be) available to defray some of the service charge costs it should not be brought into account in calculating the level of the service charge.

3.27 Sinking funds and reserves

3.28 With a view to securing so far as may reasonably be practicable that the service charge should be progressive and cumulative rather than irregular and that tenants for the time being shall bear a proper part of accumulating liabilities which accrue in the future the Landlord is entitled to include as an item of service charge for any service charge period an amount which the Landlord reasonably determines is appropriate to build up and maintain a sinking fund and a reserve fund in accordance with the principles of good estate management

3.29 Any such sinking fund is to be established and maintained on normal commercial principles for the renewal and replacement of lifts plants machinery and equipment in the Building

3.30 Any such reserve fund is to be established and maintained to cover prospective and contingent costs carrying out repairs decoration maintenance and renewals and of complying with statutes by-laws regulations of all competent authorities and of the insurers in relation to the use occupation and enjoyment of the Building

3.27–
3.30

The theory behind sinking (or reserve) funds is that they are intended to enable large capital items of service charge expenditure (which do not tend to occur annually by virtue of the nature) to be spread over the term of the lease. They can also cover items of a periodically recurring nature such as decoration of common parts, exterior maintenance etc. The main advantages of such funds are that landlords will have funds readily available to pay for large items of capital expenditure for major works, tenants are not required to pay particularly large amounts in any one year, and tenants enjoy the comfort of knowing that all works which need to be done can be done and that funds are available to undertake them.

However, despite the compelling theoretical arguments in favour of sinking funds, there are major tax disadvantages, tenants often feel aggrieved at contributing towards items of expenditure from which they actually derive no benefit (because a tenant has passed his Lease on) and such funds are often at risk to landlord's creditors, although this latter point can be overcome by proper drafting. In addition, management and administration of such funds can prove to be a real headache for the landlord. If, however, landlords insist on such funds, it is important to bear in mind that a number of the difficulties can be overcome by proper drafting. Ideally, leases should not oblige the landlord to maintain such a fund but should give him the option to do so and it should also be made clear that any tax liability flowing from the fund should be met out of the fund. The tenant should ensure that funds are kept in a separate account (ring fenced and kept secure from landlord's creditors). The aims and purpose of the fund should be made absolutely clear and any funds in the sinking fund at the end of the Lease term should be returned to the then current tenants. One other consideration to consider is whether the fund is to be held on trust (albeit that this can have adverse tax advantages) and if so, the beneficiaries should be identified as those tenants from time to time in occupation of the property. Sinking funds are too complicated and involved to be covered fully here an in the event that the landlords are insistent upon its inclusion further research should be undertaken.

SCHEDULE 7 – THE SUBJECTIONS

Those matters referred to in the register of title number [~~CW 875823~~] as evidenced by office copy entries of the said title number dated the day of 20[ ]

SCHEDULE 7 – THE SUBJECTIONS

In an attempt to crystallise those matters to which the building is subject and subject to which, therefore, the tenant takes the premises, it is important to crystallise this by setting out the date of office copy entries on which the tenant is relying. The author would suggest that these office copy entries or at least certified copies are in fact kept with the deeds following completion of the lease.

SCHEDULE 8 – THE AUTHORISED GUARANTEE AGREEMENT

DATE [   ]

PARTIES

1.	*'Guarantor'*	[(name of outgoing tenant)] [of (address) (or as appropriate) the registered office of which is at (address)] [Company Registration number [ ]]
2.	*'Landlord'*	[(name of landlord)] [of (address) (or as appropriate) the registered office of which is at (address)] [Company Registration number [ ]]

OPERATIVE PROVISIONS

1   DEFINITIONS AND INTERPRETATION

For all purposes of this guarantee the terms defined in this clause have the meanings specified

1.1	*'Assignee'*	(insert name of incoming tenant)
1.2	*'Lease'*	the lease dated (date) and made between (name of original landlord) and (name of original tenant) and (name of original guarantor) for a term of (number) years commencing on and including (commencement date) [and varied by a deed dated (date) and made between (names of parties)]
1.3	**'Premises'**	the premises demised by the Lease
1.4	*'Liability Period'*	the period during which the Assignee is bound by the tenant covenants of the Lease

1.5   *Terms from the Landlord and Tenant (Covenants) Act 1995*

The expressions 'authorised guarantee agreement' and 'tenant covenants' have the same meaning in this guarantee as in the Landlord and Tenant (Covenants) Act 1995 section 28(1)

1.6   *References to clauses*

Any reference in this deed to a clause without further designation is to be construed as a reference to the clause of this deed so numbered

SCHEDULE 8 – THE AUTHORISED GUARANTEE AGREEMENT

With a small number of relatively minor and outdated exceptions, any commercial lease granted after 1 January 1996 takes effect as a *new tenancy* as defined by the Landlord and Tenant (Covenants) Act 1995. A tenant is automatically released from liability under the tenant's covenants contained in the lease on any assignment of the lease (unless it is an *excluded assignment*, as defined in the 1995 Act) but to give the landlord some comfort, the 1995 Act introduced Authorised Guarantee Agreements (widely known now as 'AGAs') to ensure landlords could require, as a condition of giving consent to an assignment, that the assignor should guarantee the performance of the tenant's covenants until the assignee is himself released following a lawful assignment thereby compensating the landlord for and the loss of the original tenant's liability and the privity of contract principle applicable to an old lease (ie a lease granted before 1 January 1996). Section 16(2) of the 1995 Act sets out three requirements which must be satisfied for such an Agreement to be regarded as an AGA:

- it must be an agreement under which the tenant guarantees the performance by the assignee of the relevant tenant's covenants from which the tenant is to be released;

- it must be entered into in circumstances set out in s 3 of the 1995 Act; and

- its provisions must conform with s 16(4) and (5) of the 1995 Act.

AGAs can be lawfully imposed in two circumstances:

1. where the Lease specifies for the purpose of s 19(1)(a) of the Landlord and Tenant Act 1927 that the tenant is to enter into an AGA as a condition of consent to any Assignment; or

2. where it is otherwise reasonable to impose the condition. The AGA must comply with s 16(4) of the 1995 Act, and may not impose on the tenant any requirement to guarantee the performance of the relevant tenant's covenants by any person other than the assignee, nor may it impose on the tenant any liability restriction or other requirement in relation to any time after the assignee is himself released from the tenant's covenants by virtue of the 1995 Act. The obvious circumstance when this is likely to happen is when the assignee itself assigns the Lease.

From a landlord's point of view, and given the very strict requirements contained in s 16(4) and the complication of excluded assignments referred to in the 1995 Act, it is useful to define clearly the duration of the tenant''s guarantee in the AGA. A landlord's solicitor must also be conscious of the fact that there are still several unresolved issues in relation to what is permitted in relation to AGAs and what is not. Certain provisions in AGAs may well be found by the courts to go beyond what is permitted. The landlords may, therefore, wish to draft such obligations allowing for severance, trying to keep any guarantor's covenants in an AGA separate from the tenant's covenants by using a

2   RECITALS

2.1   *Consent required*

By clause (insert number) of the Lease, the Landlord's consent to an assignment of the Lease is required

2.2   *Agreement to consent*

The Landlord has agreed to give consent to the assignment to the Assignee on condition that the Guarantor enters into this guarantee

2.3   *Effective time*

This guarantee takes effect only when the Lease is assigned to the Assignee

3   GUARANTOR'S COVENANTS

In consideration of the Landlord's consent to the assignment, the Guarantor covenants with the Landlord and without the need for any express assignment with all his successors in title as set out in this clause 3

3.1   *Payment and performance*

The Assignee must punctually pay the rents reserved by the Lease and observe and perform the covenants and other terms of it throughout the Liability Period, and if at any time during the Liability Period the Assignee defaults in paying the rents or in observing or performing any of the covenants or other terms of the Lease the Guarantor must pay the rents and observe or perform the covenants or terms in respect of which the Assignee is in default, and make good to the Landlord on demand, ~~and indemnify the Landlord against,~~ all reasonable foreseeable losses, damages, costs and expenses resulting from such non-payment non-performance or non-observance notwithstanding:

3.1.1   any time or indulgence granted by the Landlord to the Assignee, or any neglect or forbearance of the Landlord in enforcing the payment of the rents or the observance or per-formance of the covenants or other terms of the Lease, or any refusal by the Landlord to accept rents tendered by or on behalf of the Assignee at a time when the Landlord is entitled, or will after the service of a notice under the Law of Property Act 1925 section 146 be entitled, to re-enter the Premises

blue pencil type of clause. It is also vitally important to note the Code's new recommendation regarding the requirement for AGAs. The recommendation (recommendation 9) urges landlords to '...*consider requiring Authorised Guarantee Agreements only where the Assignee is of lower financial standing of the Assignor or at the date of the Assignment*'. This of course confirms every instinct of common sense that most draftsmen have, but is certainly not current practice.

3.1.2   that the terms of the Lease may have been varied by agreement between the parties <u>unless the variation is prejudicial to
the Guarantor</u>

3.1.3   that the Assignee has surrendered part of the Premises, in
which event the liability of the Guarantor under the Lease is to
continue in respect of the part of the Premises not surrendered
after making any necessary apportionments under the Law of
Property Act 1925 section 146 and

3.1.4   anything else by which, but for this clause 3.1, the Guarantor
would have been released

3.2   *New lease following disclaimer*

If, during the Liability Period, any trustee in bankruptcy or liquidator of the Assignee disclaims the Lease, the Guarantor
must, if required by notice served by the Landlord within ~~6~~30
days of the Landlord's becoming aware of the disclaimer, take
from the Landlord forthwith a lease of the Premises for the
residue of the contractual term of the Lease as at the date of
the disclaimer, at the rent then being paid under the Lease and
subject to the same covenants and terms as in the Lease the
new lease to commence on the date of the disclaimer. The
Guarantor must pay the <u>reasonable and proper </u>costs of the
new lease and execute and deliver to the Landlord a counterpart of it

3.3   *Payments following disclaimer*

If, during the Liability Period, the Lease is disclaimed and for
any reason the Landlord does not require the Guarantor to
accept a new lease of the Premises in accordance with clause
3.2, the Guarantor must pay to the Landlord on demand an
amount equal to the rents reserved by the Lease for the period commencing with the date of the disclaimer and ending on
whichever is the earlier of the date being ~~6~~3 months after the
disclaimer the date, if any, on which the Premises are relet,
and the end of the contractual term of the Lease<u> and the
Landlord covenants to use his best endeavours to relet the
same</u>

4   LANDLORD'S COVENANT

4.1   The Landlord covenants with the Guarantor that he will notify
the Guarantor in writing within 7 days of being informed of
the facts bringing the Liability Period to an end<u> and will repay
to the Guarantor (with interest) any sum paid for a period
beyond the date on which the Liability Period comes to an end</u>

5   SEVERANCE

5.1   *Severance of void provisions*

Any provision of this deed rendered void by virtue of the Landlord and Tenant (Covenants) Act 1995 section 25 is to be severed from all remaining provisions, and the remaining provisions are to be preserved

5.2   *Limitation of provisions*

If any provision in this deed extends beyond the limits permitted by the Landlord and Tenant (Covenants) Act 1995 section 25, that provision is to be varied so as not to extend beyond those limits

IN WITNESS whereof the parties hereto have executed this deed the date first hereinbefore written

Original/

The Common Seal of [   ]   )

Limited was hereunto affixed in the presence   )

of:–   )

....

Director

....

Secretary/Director

Counterpart/

The Common Seal of [   ]   )

Limited was hereunto affixed in the presence   )

of:–   )

....

Director

....

Secretary/Director

Index

[all references are to page number]